# *COMICAL SPIRIT OF SEVENTY-SIX*

Fras. Hopkinson

# *COMICAL SPIRIT OF SEVENTY-SIX: The Humor of Francis Hopkinson*

*Edited with an Introduction by PAUL M. ZALL*

*THE HUNTINGTON LIBRARY*
*SAN MARINO, CALIFORNIA*
*1976*

San Marino, California
Library of Congress Catalog Card Number 75–12005
ISBN 0–87328–067–9
Designed by Neysa Moss
Printed in the United States of America by Kingsport Press

*For Andy and April*

# CONTENTS

# LIST OF ILLUSTRATIONS



Unless otherwise indicated, illustrations are from material in the Huntington collections.

# *COMICAL SPIRIT OF SEVENTY-SIX*

# INTRODUCTION

This first modern edition of comical works by Francis Hopkinson is intended to help revive a spirit that graced our nation at its birth. In the crucial period between the convening of the first Continental Congress in 1774 and the ratification of the Constitution in 1789, Hopkinson played the role later to be assumed by such national jesters as Will Rogers and Art Buchwald—relieving the tensions of an anxious age with an effervescent mixture of tomfoolery and common sense. While his contemporary writers argued for revolution and federalism with sermons or harsh satires, Hopkinson used fantasy and good humor that appealed alike to radicals, conservatives, and the vast undecided majority in between whose support proved decisive in the end. Midway in the war, when British marauders went out of their way to lay waste his home, he received it as a tribute to his powers: "I have not Abilities to assist our righteous Cause by personal Prowess & Force of Arms, but I have done it all the Service I could with my Pen."[1] He had been kept out of combat by his tiny size (John Adams described his head as "not bigger than a large Apple"),[2] but what he lacked in heroic deeds was made up in words that inspired his countrymen to go on with a war they thought would never end. And when at last the war did end, his good humor and good sense lightened the darkest hours of the emerging nation.

1. George E. Hastings, *Life & Works of Francis Hopkinson* (Chicago, 1926), p. 277.
2. L. H. Butterfield, ed., *Adams Family Correspondence*, 2 vols. (Cambridge, Mass., 1963), 2:104.

If today too few know Francis Hopkinson it is because his comic spirit has slept for two hundred years, deep in the files of the newspapers of his time. Selections of his work that sometimes appear in textbooks come not from those files but from a collection of his *Miscellaneous Essays* (1792), far different from the writings his contemporaries first read. In a deliberate attempt to elevate his earlier works above their rude origins in the popular press, he had polished and bowdlerized them all, suppressing the lively roughshod spirit that had been their true strength. So as to restore that spirit, this edition presents the best of Hopkinson's comic works as they first appeared in rough-and-ready dress, modernizing only typography and editorial conventions, and adding commentary for the convenience of modern readers who would wish to meet Hopkinson as his contemporaries knew him. We begin, then, with a broad assessment of his personality and accomplishment, postponing the details for the introductory commentaries intended to display the works in the context of their times.

By some happy accident of history, Hopkinson's career coincided with the dramatic development of America as a newspaper-reading nation. He was not a practicing newspaperman, but rather a multi-talented gentleman of modest means and boundless energy, busily pursuing the various projects that led to his signing the Declaration of Independence, composing America's first secular songs, designing the Stars and Stripes, inventing a metronome, and suffering as the first American judge to be impeached. In that busy life, dashing off essays to the press was a necessary means to promoting his projects, and he followed the rule of his lifelong friend Benjamin Franklin, who never embarked upon a philanthropic venture without first preparing "the Minds of the People by writing on the Subject in the Newspapers."[3] When Franklin transferred this technique to preparing the minds of the people for revolution, Hopkinson followed faithfully.

---

3. Benjamin Franklin, *Autobiography*, ed. L. W. Labaree (New Haven, 1964), p. 200.

By that time, Franklin had helped to develop a national press and a nation of readers who now reacted less as colonists and more as Americans. In Hopkinson's youth nearly half the space in a local newspaper would have consisted of local news and advertising, the other half of reprints from the British press. Citizens of Philadelphia thus knew more about what was happening in Cornwall than about what was going on in North Carolina. Franklin had helped to change the scope, content, and influence of American newspapers, chiefly through his own practice in *Poor Richard's Almanac* and the *Pennsylvania Gazette*—with "Poor Richard" appealing to common people, who scarcely read anything else, and the columns of the *Gazette* to more learned readers, including those raised to that rank through the *Almanac.* Franklin also entered partnerships with former apprentices as they set up shops along the seaboard and into the frontier, providing capital and counsel, and then, as postmaster general, establishing a swift, efficient postal system that made an intercolonial news service possible for a national press. Thus, on the eve of the Revolution, when Hopkinson launched his career in political propaganda, he could be confident of being read on the farthest frontiers. Fifteen years later, as he closed that career, the number of newspapers in America had increased from about forty to well over sixty, as many in proportion to the population as there would be on the eve of World War II.[4] This unbridled growth had its dangers, since the press could carry counterpropaganda in wartime and irresponsible libel in peace, but in promoting his program of political and cultural change Hopkinson found a national press ideal.

Given this scope, he appealed to a broad spectrum of readers. With a fine talent for parody, he could imitate Addison and Steele for the genteel, Swift or Sterne for the middle class, Franklin for apprentices and farmers—or any other popular model who could be turned to the purposes of propaganda. In the custom

4. Arthur M. Schlesinger, *Prelude to Independence* (New York, 1958), p. 296; Philip Davidson, *Propaganda & the American Revolution* (Chapel Hill, 1941), p. 235; and Frank Luther Mott, *American Journalism*, 3rd ed. (New York, 1962), pp. 113, 115.

of the day, he wrote anonymously and switched styles so skillfully that even newspaper publishers might not know who had written the work he sent them. Sometimes he would promote one argument and then, under a different pseudonym, demolish it in the next edition. This could have been harmless fun another time, but in an age when newspaper warfare was waged in dead earnest, the act of writing on politics incurred the risk of brutal retaliation, and Hopkinson early learned that a press powerful enough to mold national opinion could also destroy private character. Nevertheless, he was driven by a sense of cultural mission and zeal for the nationalism that would make a new culture possible, and he ran the risk of character assassination even though a good name was his only hedge against financial ruin.

His sense of mission and his good name had come to him, along with £900, as a legacy from his father, Thomas Hopkinson, who had been one of Franklin's "Junto," the small band of enterprising young men who had dedicated their lives to doing good. Francis was in fact the first fruit of the Junto's plan to educate young Americans toward a culture that would some day surpass Britain's, since it would be rooted in the humanist tradition but would also draw sustenance from modern science and technology. Thomas Hopkinson had served with Franklin as a founding trustee of the academy they established as a seedbed for this culture, and his son had been the first to be enrolled. The academy soon grew to a college, and Francis Hopkinson was in the first graduating class, but his father did not live to see him through, dying in 1751 at the age of forty-two. The obituary Franklin wrote for the *Pennsylvania Gazette* told how Judge Hopkinson had overcome a painful shyness (inherited by his son) to make his way in the world from an obscure scrivener's shop to a succession of highly sensitive judicial posts where he combined "the Wisdom of a Philosopher" with "the innocence of a Child" (14 November 1751). He left the bulk of his comfortable estate to his widow so that she could raise their six children to fulfill the dream they shared of a new culture on America's shores.

Mary Johnson Hopkinson fulfilled her husband's wishes with a little help from Franklin and marvelous management of her own. Three of her four daughters wed cultivated young men, and the fourth chose to remain with her mother in the heart of Philadelphia's lively culture. The younger son entered training to become an Episcopalian minister, and only the eldest child, Francis, gave her any trouble. After graduating, then studying law with the provincial attorney general and passing the bar, he still felt too diffident, too easily discouraged by competition, to practice law and much preferred to practice the organ instead. His moral character was fine and his disposition lively, but Mrs. Hopkinson worried because he could not decide on a choice of life.

For a while he tried writing. As an undergraduate he had shown some talent in genteel verses commemorating the death of George II and then the accession of George III, and as an alumnus he wrote commencement odes for the college every year, all of which appeared in the newspapers to popular acclaim. He was thus encouraged to publish as a pamphlet a long poem praising the college education he had received, dedicating it to every member of the faculty and of the first graduating class by name. Entitled *Science,* the poem concluded with a rousing prophecy of a new culture when "Fair Science" should soften "with reforming Hand/ The native rudeness of a barbarous Land," and proved so popular that it was immediately pirated.

Only a week after *Science* appeared, Hopkinson was advertising a warning to beware a spurious edition filled with "gross Errors" and "Absurdities" published by Philadelphia's leading Presbyterian printer, Andrew Steuart. But Hopkinson's advertisement appeared directly above Steuart's own advertisement offering the pamphlet at one-sixth the list price—even less if purchased in large lots (*Pennsylvania Gazette* 18 March 1762). And a month later, the *New York Mercury* reprinted Hopkinson's warning as a part of what had been Steuart's advertisement but now carried the name of Hugh Gaine of New York as publisher. The copyright law of the time offered no help against this flagrant piracy, so Hopkinson suffered in silence until Steuart published a Latin grammar for the college.

Then Hopkinson rushed into print with a list of 151 mistakes to be found in Steuart's 137 pages, but Steuart merely shrugged it off with a pamphlet entitled *Ass in the Lyon's Skin*—the title alluding to both the Aesop fable and the fact that Hopkinson's latest project was a collection of psalm tunes to compete with those earlier collected by James Lyon. Steuart otherwise left the debate to the college faculty who had been responsible for proofreading the grammar. They showed that Hopkinson's criticism was of no importance, and that the only Latin words he had used, he had misused. He replied in manuscript verses that circulated on the campus satirizing the "learned professors" as asses. They retaliated with similar satire, but written in Latin, mocking his psalm tunes—"What a novelty surpasses the marvels of old bards,/ Now a dull ass composes songs."[5]

Apparently caught up in the excitement of pamphleteering, Hopkinson now turned to take on two-thirds of the population of Pennsylvania with an attack on Presbyterians, Baptists, and Quakers who had raised objections to a project of his, promoting instrumental music during church services. But as soon as his pamphlet, *The Lawfulness of Instrumental Musick,* was advertised in the *Gazette* for 28 April 1763, there also appeared an advertisement for a "Second Edition" published by Steuart, except that this time the "Second Edition" was not a reprint but a parody, ridiculing Hopkinson's pamphlet and his passion for the organ. Worse, it raised the specter of scandal, for a concluding note alluded not only to his tiny physique but to the entertaining probability that he had been consorting with an actress: "The ingenious Francis Hopkinson, ESQUIRE, stood so high in the good Graces of Mrs. *Douglass,* and the rest of the strolling Stage-Players, that HE prevailed on them to perform a Play, the profits arising therefrom, purchased the College Organ."

---

5. Thomas P. Haviland, "Francis Hopkinson and the Grammarians," *PMHB,* 76 (1952), 65–66.

Hopkinson had indeed persuaded the players to give a benefit performance that had enabled the college to buy an organ, but the slightest hint that there had been anything between him and Mrs. Douglass could be read as covert blackmail, a warning to keep quiet or risk his reputation. A gentleman of his modest means could hardly afford that risk, since he had to husband his good name if he wished to follow the common course for young men in his position—marrying a wealthy heiress of reputable family. Such a warning was sufficient to discourage a writing career, and Hopkinson kept quiet for the next ten years.

During those ten years he searched for a way of life both genteel and secure enough to allow him to cultivate his cultural interests. Thanks to Franklin, he was appointed customs collector for the small port of Salem, New Jersey in 1763–64. There his income depended entirely on whatever customs he could collect from veteran smugglers running a lively trade in heavily taxed sugar, rum, and molasses, and Hopkinson's activity consisted of writing notices in the newspapers, warning everyone that the law said duties had to be paid on these commodities. To supplement the meager commission he was able to earn, he took on a task congenial to his tastes, adapting the Psalms for the hymnal of the Dutch Reformed Church in New York. He spent the next two years arduously adapting the common meter of the English psalter (alternating lines of eight and six syllables) to a meter more amenable to Dutch (ten-syllable couplets), all for a fee of £145. This fee, however, would enable him to seek his fortune in England when his post at Salem vanished.

That post was swamped in 1765 by widespread public agitation against the Stamp Act. As new taxes on legal paper and newspapers provoked unprecedented united action by the colonists, local customs collectors like Hopkinson became scapegoats and fled their posts in the face of rising violence. Hopkinson then opened an office in Philadelphia as a conveyancer of deeds, a venture also bound to fail since it depended upon using legal paper that was taxed and thus boycotted by patriots and those who feared retribution from patriots. Consequently, in the spring of 1765, Franklin, who had been asked to wangle an invitation for Hopkinson to visit relatives in England, had to confess that the young man of twenty-seven still lived with his mother, not having established himself in "any material Business as yet."[6]

It was at the appeal of Mrs. Hopkinson that Franklin had searched out English cousins of hers who could provide her son with some kind of security. Franklin had uncovered one cousin who could prove ideal. He was the influential James Johnson, once chaplain to George II and now the Bishop of Worcester, famous for generosity to relatives and known to be the sole support of at least seven of them. Succumbing to Franklin's perseverance, he invited Hopkinson for a year's visit.

Hopkinson set sail from Philadelphia in May 1766. On the night of his departure the city's skies blazed in celebration of the repeal of the Stamp Act, a stunning victory for the American press that had rallied Americans as Americans to apply pressure on British agents until, with a change of ministry in London, Parliament had capitulated. Thus Hopkinson sailed off to the mother country with great expectations reflected in the glow of a new colonial self-esteem. But the closer he came to his mother's cousin's castle, the more his innate shyness dampened those expectations. He found the castle crawling with sycophants whose fawning seemed to be more highly valued than an American cousin's obliging disposition. Too honest to use their means, he saw little to be expected from this visit except the opportunity to meet influential people who might someday be of use. Still homesick after a year's absence, he happily returned to Philadelphia in the fall of 1767, and followed Franklin's advice to take up shopkeeping.

He opened a drygoods store that also sold port wine, and within a year prospered enough to take a wife, beautiful Ann Borden, heiress of Joseph Borden, the leading citizen of Bordentown, New Jersey. For four years, Hopkinson continued to

---

6. Benjamin Franklin, *Franklin Papers,* ed. L. W. Labaree (New Haven, 1959– ), 20:125.

prosper, tending his shop, indulging his passion for music, raising a family. But by 1771 the American press had whipped up renewed agitation against Parliament's tax policies—this time against import duties on such building materials as glass and painter's lead. A series of patriotic "non-importation agreements" shut off Hopkinson's supplies, while concurrently a cartel of Quaker merchants undercut his prices and set up competing shops in his neighborhood. Facing financial disaster, he begged the aid of the proprietary governor, John Penn, whom he had met at his cousin's castle. Penn charitably gave him enough money to clear his debts, along with a little property outside of town.

At the same time, more substantial help came from another of the influential people he had met in England, the wife of Prime Minister North himself, who secured for him a political sinecure as collector of customs at New Castle, Delaware.[7] This post was far superior to the one he had held at Salem ten years earlier, for New Castle was a bustling way station between Philadelphia and Baltimore, and the port employed a large customs staff, so that the collector's presence was seldom required. The political climate there was calm, especially after the government finally repealed all duties except those on tea. Since pilots on the Delaware River refused to board ships carrying tea, none berthed at New Castle, and Hopkinson was spared the trouble brewing at Boston.

In his new prosperity, then, he moved his little family to Bordentown, to a comfortably large house across the road from his wife's ancestral home. There, a country gentleman relieved from the need to earn a living, he launched his career in politics. In a colony where the governor was William Franklin, Benjamin's son, and in a county where Joseph Borden was baron, Hopkinson's rise was sure and swift. He was named justice of the peace for the county and, in April 1774, a member of the prestigious Governor's Council. He had been writing squibs for his father-

7. Unpublished letter, Huntington manuscript EM 39.

in-law's personal quarrels and so had become fair game for local satirists, who greeted his appointments with scurrilous comments about the *"pretty, little, musical, poetical witling"* soaring to power on a bridal veil (*Pennsylvania Packet,* 11 April 1774). But Hopkinson's concerns now transcended petty personal politics and he would not stoop to reply.

Parliament's harsh repression of Boston in the spring of 1774 provided the radicals one more proof of the need for American autonomy, and when, in the course of the summer, a call went out for a Continental Congress to plan concerted action, Hopkinson popularized their arguments in a sprightly pamphlet called *A Pretty Story.* It told a tale of the foul deeds perpetrated on a hardy band of pioneers far from their father's farm by their stepmother and her steward—bringing the parable down to the closing of Boston Port and leaving the conclusion to depend on the pioneers' next move. The pamphlet appeared in three editions between August and the close of the year, but Hopkinson also had more practical politics on his mind. Angered by the conservative stand taken by New Jersey's delegates to the first Congress, he and his fellow radicals set about ensuring that their own voices would be heard in the second.

On the eve of the second Congress, they finally gained control of the Governor's Council as well as of the Assembly, and hastily revised the constitution, enabling them to elect representatives of their own. With Hopkinson in the van, the new delegation hurried down to Philadelphia in time to swing the vote for the Declaration of Independence. And though that measure put his patrons, the governors, out of office and dissolved his sinecure, Hopkinson burned with a patriotic zeal for the Revolution that consumed his interests for the next half-dozen years. From 1776 to mid-summer 1778, he headed the vital Navy Board with powers equivalent to those of a secretary of the navy, and for the next three years he tackled the really impossible task of managing the national debt, trying to keep track of interest and payments on loans from allies in a day when even ardent patriots had no confidence in Congressional currency.

Yet, despite these wracking duties, he somehow found time to write as if he had been a practicing journalist. During 1775–76, while the political pot had bubbled in New Jersey, he had tossed off a half-dozen sprightly essays, light social satire, for the *Pennsylvania Magazine,* edited by his neighbor Tom Paine until wartime shortages put it out of business. After that, every year saw at least three or four political satires along with countless (because anonymous) serious pieces, all adjusted to patriotic expediency. He aimed his satires first at homebred Tories because he saw them as a subversive threat capable of undermining the new government; and then at the British forces whose presence was awesome until Hopkinson pilloried their leaders on parodies of their own proclamations. When the British occupied Philadelphia in the winter of 1777–78, he went into exile with the government, of course, but so did the friendly newspapers—the *Gazette* and the *Packet*—for which he had been writing since the demise of the *Pennsylvania Magazine,* and so he was able to publish vigorously as ever, a brilliant beacon for American patriots in their darkest hour.

In one instance his official and artistic lives coalesced. As chairman of the Navy Board, he perpetrated a masterful feat of psychological warfare by floating a few waterproofed kegs of gunpowder from Bordentown down the Delaware River to Philadelphia harbor where they served as mines, putting the British occupation troops into such panic that they subsequently shot at anything afloat—or so said the ballad Hopkinson published, "The Battle of the Kegs." Neither the ballad nor the newspaper accounts of this explosive event said anything about the fact that the kegs had been fabricated by his father-in-law or that the plan had been Hopkinson's own. It was enough for him that the ballad proved popular and lifted morale when at its lowest ebb. (He would have delighted in knowing that the ballad was sung again in 1969, and that an enterprising Marine lieutenant re-created the feat it celebrated by floating kegs down the Mekong Delta during the Viet Nam conflict.)

As the Revolutionary War wound down, Hopkinson turned his

satiric sights on those Tories allowed to roam freely in Philadelphia, where they threatened internal security, even breaking into the State House to steal congressional secret papers. Worse were those who maintained regular traffic with Tories exiled in New York. There they conducted regular counterinsurgency raids, sending bands of marauders to terrorize New Jersey, counterfeiting Continental money, spreading false rumors, and waging a full-scale propaganda war to undermine public support for Washington's goal of unconditional surrender by the British forces. Hopkinson hit the Tories with squib upon squib, but to no avail. Public officials who could have curbed them went complacently on indulging their claims to postwar prosperity and political position. His voice cried in a wilderness: "Most of our Writers," he complained to Franklin, "have left the great Field of general Politics . . . to skirmish & bush-fight in the Fens & Thickets of Party Dispute. . . ."[8]

Hopkinson himself fell into party disputes aplenty, but, for the immediate postwar years, kept them apart from his satires. In 1780 he was appointed judge of the Admiralty Court, a post similar to one his father had held with honor decades before. Politically this appointment was amazing because it came from George Bryan, political boss of Pennsylvania and Hopkinson's sworn political enemy. Bryan's party of Presbyterians called themselves Constitutionalists because they were sworn to uphold the state constitution (not to be confused with the later Federal Constitution that they would violently oppose). Bryan had designed the constitution to ensure that his party, though a minority in numbers, would control the state government. By virtue of one provision, any citizen desiring to hold property or public office or even to vote had first to take a loyalty oath forswearing all enemies, past and present, of the Revolution. Quakers found any oath anathema on religious grounds, and many Episcopalians found this one intolerable because it meant renouncing friends and relatives who had chosen to remain British subjects. Thus

8. Hastings, p. 279.

this so-called Test Act had decimated the Episcopalian-Quaker coalition that had ruled Pennsylvania before the war. Now Hopkinson and a small group of friends formed an opposition party, calling themselves Republicans, dedicated to defeating Bryan, repealing his Test Act, and making the constitution more democratic. In view of this, Bryan's naming Hopkinson to the bench was like inviting the fox to tend the henhouse.

Bryan's motive is now unfathomable, but whatever he intended, he placed Hopkinson high in state government for a seven-year term (renewed at the end of that term when the Republicans assumed control). In the Admiralty Court Judge Hopkinson, like his father before him, was charged with deciding claims and counterclaims, often of a highly sensitive kind. Many of his cases related to British ships captured as prizes of war, making him vulnerable to charges of favoritism and, since his fees derived from commissions, venality. By the end of his first year he was impeached by the assembly for allegedly offering a citizen a post in return for a suit of clothes (and then appointing someone else); accepting a bribe of a cask of wine; and illegally authorizing the sale of a prize ship. When the case reached the state supreme court it was thrown out at once, but only after having acquired a widespread publicity that would haunt Hopkinson's future.

For the moment, however, his recourse was to his muse, and he expressed his rage in manuscript verses reminiscent of those he had written about the college professors in his youth. Now he confided to his notebook an allegory about a dog named "Chance" and a lawyer named "Skunk" who team up to ruin the household cat. The dog had been dismissed from the house for upsetting the parlor,

> And yelping creep'd beneath a ruin'd Shed
> To hide his Head:
> There on a Dung heap sat
> Whining,
> Repining,
> And cursing his hard Fate.

The skunk persuades him to seek vengeance on the cat who now enjoys the family's favor alone. They falsely accuse her of upsetting the parlor, but "Puss" is quickly acquitted and their villainy exposed. Unpublished, this saga remained in Hopkinson's notebook, perhaps because such personal satire was felt to be beneath a judge's dignity.

Despite their political differences, Hopkinson served Bryan well, for by virtue of his judicial post he also sat on the state's supreme court and on the High Court of Errors and Appeals, a sort of super-supreme court that monitored government operations as a whole. In addition, his office entitled him to a place on the Board of Trustees of what was now the University of Pennsylvania, after the charter of the college had been revoked because the previous board (of which Hopkinson had also been a member) had shown too little zeal for the Revolution. Bryan, nominally vice-president of the state's Executive Council, sat alongside him on these various courts and boards, where (in the absence of rumor to the contrary) we must assume they got along famously.

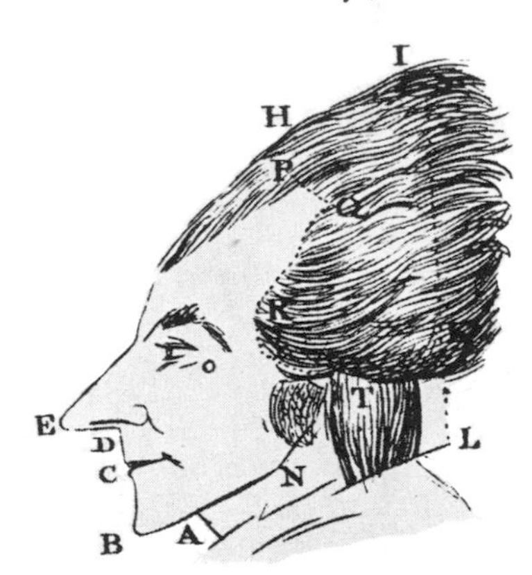


At least Hopkinson seldom satirized Bryan in the newspapers. His best effort in this respect was a connect-the-dots puzzle which, when filled out, was said to be a caricature of George Bryan shaping Pennsylvania in his own physiognomy. Hopkinson treated the Bryan-controlled assembly with similar whimsy. One satire featured a wooden post delivering a legislative oration against a recent ordinance banishing trees from the streets of Philadelphia. Inspired by the post's speech, public reaction forced repeal from an assembly that normally would listen only to George Bryan.

Hopkinson's satire was not restricted to local politics. When Congress, frightened by a mob of veterans demanding back pay, fled Philadelphia, they regrouped at Princeton. There they found the site too small and too inconvenient, so they voted to hold alternate sessions at new sites to be selected near Trenton in the north and Annapolis in the south. Hopkinson greeted this decision with a proposal that they build an assembly hall upon a huge pendulum that would swing back and forth from site to site. When this plan received no congressional response, he proposed another by which they would meet in an enormous wooden horse, mounted on wheels so that it could be trundled up and down the Delaware shores.

This kind of whimsy was in calculated contrast to the tone of other postwar political essays in the newspapers. Franklin congratulated him for ignoring those "Pieces of Abuse" that had been clogging Philadelphia papers. These had grown so noisome that Franklin feared for the image they created of American civilization and so would censor the newspapers that he passed on to his Parisian friends. He took the occasion to lecture Hopkinson on the responsibility of a newspaper publisher to consider himself "in some degree the Guardian of his Country's Reputation, and refuse to insert such Writings as may hurt it." If people insisted on abusing one another in print, "let them do it in little Pamphlets"—"It is absurd to trouble all the world with . . . Matters so unprofitable and so disagreeable."[9]

Hopkinson hardly needed to be told that. In one of his wartime satires he himself had made the same point another way, having a Tory lament the freedom of the press and the pen: "It is true they break no bones and shed no blood, but they can instigate others to do both; and, by influencing the minds of the multitude, can perhaps do more towards gaining a point than the best rifle gun or the sharpest bayonet." The press that had helped to create a nation could also undermine it at home and abroad. And now Hopkinson saw the newspapers increasingly being used for perpetuating petty quarrels that degenerated into vile name calling

---

9. Benjamin Franklin, *The Writings of Benjamin Franklin,* ed. Albert Henry Smyth, 10 vols. (New York, 1905–07), 8:647–48.

contests ("liar," "rascal," "s---poke"). Their numbers too were increasing: an estimated sixty new newspapers began publishing in the mid-eighties,[10] and with greater frequency also. In September 1784, the *Pennsylvania Packet* began daily publication with such success that others followed. And from this turmoil Hopkinson could not long stand aloof, for he himself became a popular target of newspaper abuse.

When unconditional surrender came at last, Hopkinson sent off two hilarious squibs at James Rivington, long the fountainhead of Tory propaganda in America. A prosperous bookseller and publisher of the court-subsidized *New York Royal Gazette,* Rivington still carried on scot-free with *Rivington's Gazette.* For the *Packet,* then, Hopkinson composed a public notice that Rivington would hold a "going out of business sale" and included a catalog of bogus books whose titles celebrated British defeats on land and sea and in diplomacy. The next week he published a mock reply from Rivington complaining about the notice and protesting that he had always been a true patriot. To Hopkinson's surprise, Rivington had friends in Philadelphia who counterattacked in Rivington's paper with a travesty of the cantata, "The Temple of Minerva," which Hopkinson had produced in honor of Washington. They called their version "The Temple of Cloacina," printing it in parallel columns with excerpts from the original that lent themselves to scatological parody.

With good-humored detachment, Hopkinson replied with a lively tale of traveling across darkest Philadelphia in search of a copy of Rivington's paper. The only copy he could find, having been used for toilet tissue, slipped out of his grasp and was lost for good. Rivington reprinted the opening paragraph of that tale with a new version ("second edition") even more scatological than the travesty had been—as an example of patriot belles-lettres. Hopkinson's patriot defenders rushed to his defense, hurling turd for turd as they came, until, above his own signature, he asked Rivington for a truce. Rivington mocked the gesture and

10. Mott, p. 113.

the patriots exploded, more at Hopkinson for making the appeal than at Rivington for rejecting it. Led by the *Freeman's Journal* and then the *Independent Gazetteer,* the rabidly patriotic press would watch him warily for the next ten years of his life.

Their attacks struck at his patriotism, his personality, even his purse. His overture to Rivington reminded extremist patriots about the old friendship with ex-Governor William Franklin who was now exiled in New York where, it was alleged, he masterminded the counterinsurgency raids against New Jersey and thus made Hopkinson culpable by old association. That recollection in turn brought to mind Hopkinson's penchant for attaching himself to the wealthy and powerful, regardless of party, and they conjectured in print about the attachment being homosexual. They raised questions about his moral integrity, resurrecting the record of his impeachment and questioning his qualifications for serving in his various public posts. Ironically, those posts were pinching his private purse, since on an income that seldom rose over 500 pounds a year he could not hope to educate his five children as he himself had been educated, but his dignity as a judge prevented his engaging in trade of any kind. Still, the newspaper satirists hinted at his venality, and watched him very closely.

His dignity also kept him from counterattacking on his own behalf, but once he tried curbing the scurrility of *Le Courier de l'Amerique,* America's first French newspaper, then only two months old and already notorious for vicious attacks on the government of France, our closest ally. As a trustee of the University, he wrote to the *Pennsylvania Packet* under a favorite pseudonym, "A.B.," accusing the *Courier* of un-American activities in subverting the Franco-American alliance. He warned that newspapers had "the most direct access to the minds of the people" and thus such irresponsibility as the *Courier* displayed could weaken the alliance at home as well as in the French court. He focused his complaint on the *Courier's* mocking remarks about a large collection of French books that Louis XVI, in a magnanimous gesture, had just donated to the University. And he reported the abominable conduct of the *Courier's* editors when a respectable trustee of the University asked them to print a more accurate estimate of the collection—one he had already written for them. The respectable trustee even offered to pay for the insertion if necessary. But editor Boinod refused to publish it without the author's name. The author refused to sign it. Boinod remained recalcitrant. Thus, "A.B." had turned to the *Packet* which had freely printed the review and the prefatory letter (10 August 1784).

But in its next issue the *Packet* also printed Boinod's side of the story, including a re-creation of the impacted interview in which the respectable trustee is identified as Judge Hopkinson and Boinod as the champion of a free press:

> "I cannot," said he, "insert your complimentary paragraph unless it be signed."
>
> "But why? our American papers never refuse such things: you are bound to do it." . . .
>
> "Never shall we expose ourselves to such an infamy."
>
> "You will not insert this article," continued Mr. Hopkinson in a pet: "take care, think well on it; I will do you all the harm in my power; I will make you lose immediately five subscribers."
>
> "O sir, it is not five, a hundred or one thousand subscribers, nor any power on earth, which can intimidate or cause us to deviate from the truth—"

And thus Boinod held firm while Hopkinson fled in a pet. The *Courier* would go on attacking the French for another two months until the postmaster general imposed an exorbitant tax that put it out of business. Whether Hopkinson had anything to do with official suppression, his sally against the *Courier* was enough to reinforce the enemy's image of him as an unprincipled fool or knave or both.

For his part, Hopkinson refused to reply directly to such libels but instead kept up a good-humored burlesque of newspaper warfare on a broad front, and especially of the pathetically petty quarrels that spotted the columns of the Philadelphia press: disgruntled clients accusing lawyers of not pursuing cases with sufficient enthusiasm; musicians criticizing each other's talents; grizzled veterans disputing the prowess of others in the war. For these skirmishes, Hopkinson offered such ingenious weapons as preprinted blank forms adaptable to all arguments since they required only inserting antagonists' names and appropriate epithets; or, a sample sheet of type faces from which they could select models suited to the tone of their quarrel—the larger the letter, the louder the voice. Such nonsense laughed a quarrel or two off the pages of the press. Some quarrels succumbed to the technique Hopkinson had used with British generals in wartime, merely reprinting their own words out of context, in all their naked absurdity. But for every fool flushed out in this way, legions would leap into his place.

Hopkinson's anxiety about the quality of the press was somewhat relieved when, in 1787, two new magazines appeared in Philadelphia where there had been none since the *Pennsylvania Magazine* expired in 1776. The *Columbian Magazine* patterned itself after Britain's popular *Gentleman's Magazine* and featured miscellaneous essays, reviews, and engraved illustrations. The *American Museum* was quite different, a reprint journal, republishing pieces that had already appeared in American newspapers or pamphlets but deserved wider circulation and preservation as samples of indigenous culture. Hopkinson offered his wholehearted support, even filling in as temporary editor of the *Columbian* for two months. As editor, he promoted recent fiction and verse, and reported on the latest discoveries in science and technology, illustrating them with detailed engravings, trying hard to administer sweetness and light as an antidote to the national cultural blight engendered by the newspaper press. He also reprinted several of his wartime poems, and composed an original essay on spring cleaning in reply to one of his earlier essays on the subject that the *Museum* had reprinted in its inaugural issue. Both essays revived the urbane, sprightly wit that had brightened the *Pennsylvania Magazine,* and now seemed to signal a renaissance of good humor and philosophical calm.

But Hopkinson had one more newspaper war to wage. Though

fifty and suffering from gout, he girded his loins with the fervor of old to do battle for the Federalist cause. In September 1787 the Constitutional Convention proposed to Congress the federal system of checks and balances we have today, and Congress quickly turned the proposal over to the states for ratification. For the next six months Federalist and anti-Federalist propaganda swamped the national press. In Pennsylvania, George Bryan led the anti-Federalists, crying that the new plan would rob Americans of the God-given rights the Revolution had wrested from other tyrannical forms of government. One of his writers even hinted at treason to the Old Cause on the part of such Federalists as George Washington and Franklin, who was now head of the state's Executive Council. This charge incensed Hopkinson, for Washington was his idol and Franklin a second father.

Hopkinson counterattacked with a political allegory, "The New Roof," about the need to protect the national edifice from erosion. He tried to revive the spirit that had informed *A Pretty Story* in 1774, but his temper had thinned with age and unremitting attacks from the newspaper satirists. Towards the close of "The New Roof" his comic detachment dissolved, and he lashed out against Bryan's villainous writer, caricatured as an otherwise harmless religious fanatic whipped into a frenzy by Bryan's warnings about the impending rape of American citizens, foaming at the mouth with seditious libel. Not satisfied with that caricature, he sent a straightforward letter to the most licentious of the anti-Federalist newspapers, the *Independent Gazetteer*, paying for its insertion in order to expose the villainous writer by name and as a henchman of Bryan's in a conspiracy to libel the nation's leaders.

The anti-Federalist response was predictably swift and as scurrilous as any he had suffered in the years since Steuart's writers had silenced him a quarter-century ago, but Hopkinson endured. They accused him of being a lifelong leech on the rich and powerful, of betraying his patrons and his party for pay or public office. They caricatured his tiny body, called him a pet monkey, a homosexual, a toady, and a thief. They even threatened to reopen his impeachment at a time when, they pointed out, should the Constitution be adopted, his office would be abolished and he would have to seek another. One writer pointed out that he had never been able to make a living without someone else's help. "Scarcely a Day passes," Hopkinson sighed, "without my appearance in the Newspapers in every scandalous Garb that scribbling Vengeance can furnish."[11] It was as though his enemies had been storing up their venom for just such a time as this.

Still, he managed to regain his composure and, instead of replying in kind, began again to write the kind of good-humored parody that depended on comic detachment, leaving the anti-Federalists to drown in their own diatribes. When a newspaper publisher asked permission to reprint "The New Roof," Hopkinson gave him a version that left out the caricature in which his comic spirit had turned to gall.[12] There was no longer need to waste that spirit on anti-Federalists, since theirs had become a lost cause after June 1788 when nine of the states ratified the Constitution, making it the law of the land.

To make the Federalist victory sweeter still, Hopkinson was called upon to produce a spectacular pageant for the Fourth of July, celebrating both the Constitution and the Declaration of Independence. It was a gala day, with long lines of marchers arrayed by occupation, swirling through the streets singing a song he had written called "The New Roof," and following a float also called "The New Roof," with a wooden dome thirty-six feet high spanning thirteen columns—three left unfinished to signify states still to ratify the Constitution. That float was drawn by ten white horses to a place of honor in front of the State House where fifty-four years earlier his father and Franklin had helped lay the cornerstone. This was Hopkinson's shining hour—to him ample compensation for the years of misunderstanding, mistrust, and abuse from a people he had tried to serve so faithfully.

Exhilarated, he published a detailed description of every ele-

11. Hastings, p. 406.
12. *Columbian Magazine,* 8 (1792), 111–12.

ment in the Grand Federal Procession held on that day, and then wrote a sparkling parody of his own description, pretending that the anti-Federalists had held their own "Grand Antifederal Procession" in which all his old political enemies passed in review as skunks, dogs, and miscellaneous monsters. He kept this cathartic exercise in manuscript; having written it down, he had flushed the gall out of his system. Before the summer was over, Bryan's forces publicly conceded defeat, accepting the new Constitution as harbinger of "a new era in the American world," and thus tacitly acknowledging fulfillment of the political dream Hopkinson had spun in *A Pretty Story* fourteen years earlier.

In his last years, Hopkinson kept busy as ever, publishing a volume of secular songs dedicated to General Washington, and a collection of the decisions he had handed down in the Admiralty Court. The new Constitution abolished that court, and for a year he was once again without "any material Business" until President Washington appointed him district judge of the United States. Fifty-two and crippled now by gout, he was still able to compose music and dabble in such inventions as a device for twilling harpsichords. He served as treasurer of the American Philosophical Society until a few months before his death, and also as alderman for his ward in Philadelphia. His evenings passed most pleasantly in company with Franklin, another invalid, whose death preceded his own by one year and a month. Hopkinson suffered a serious stroke that crippled him further but still did not keep him from attending ceremonies at the University in September 1790 to receive the honorary degree of Doctor of Laws.

On 9 May 1791, he was dead at the age of 53, succumbing to a final stroke. Notwithstanding Hopkinson's long years of service to the nation and his reputation as well, the local newspapers all but ignored his passing, paying more attention to the concurrent death of a slave who had displayed a prodigious memory for mathematics. The *Packet,* for which he had written so much, reported: "Died suddenly on Monday morning last, the Hon. Francis Hopkinson, Esq. District Judge of the United States, for the state of Pennsylvania. The interests of science and patriotism, will long deplore the loss of this valuable citizen" (11 May). His old antagonist, the *Independent Gazetteer,* copied that first sentence exactly, but left out the last (14 May). A new paper, the *Mercury,* at least copied it all and added a eulogy (12 May)—

> Hopkinson! thy memory shall endure,
> As long as worth exists, or praise secure.
> With wit, law, science, every heart be warm'd;
> Whilst blended with the bard, the Patriot charm'd.

A month earlier, the *Mercury* had devoted an entire column to the obituary of George Bryan.

The only comparable obituary for Hopkinson appeared in the May issue of the *Columbian,* now called the *Universal Asylum.* Written by Dr. Benjamin Rush, who had served with Hopkinson in the Revolution and the newspaper wars, the obituary stressed his achievement in writing propaganda for his country in its time of need. Rush took for granted that his readers already knew of Hopkinson's achievements in law and science and music. But since so much of the propaganda had been anonymous, few could have realized "the irresistible influence of the *ridicule* which he poured forth" upon the enemies of revolution and, later, federalism; upon absurdities in science and education; and upon an irresponsible press:

> Newspaper scandal frequently for months together, disappeared or languished, after the publication of several of his irresistible satires. . . . He gave a currency, to a *thought* or *phrase* in these effusions from his pen, which never failed to bear down the spirit of the times, and frequently to turn the divided tides of party-rage, into one general channel of ridicule or contempt. (6:292–93)

One measure of how far Rush was right may be found in the preface to Clement Biddle's *Philadelphia Directory,* reprinted in the *Mercury* during the week that Hopkinson died.

Biddle reviewed the city's progress over the past ten years—"a very remarkable revolution in respect to the healthiness of its inhabitants" had cut the death rate dramatically. He listed a dozen factors contributing to that revolution and almost every one, at some time, had been a favorite project of Hopkinson's which he had promoted in his "irresistible satires": public sanitation, "life saving" measures, even cultivation of what we now call urban "green belts." But even more satisfying from Hopkinson's perspective was Biddle's boast of a concurrent cultural revolution, "the general diffusion of knowledge among all classes of people from our libraries, our numerous societies, monthly, weekly, and daily publications" (7 May 1791). Hopkinson had been a leader in this revolution, through energetic service for the Library Company of Philadelphia, the American Philosophical Society, and the University, as well as through his essays which he would garnish with allusions to standard authors and to recent developments in science, art, music, or literature, teasing casual readers with cultural carrots, leading them to liberal learning through laughter. Thus, as he lay dying, he could have found fulfillment of the mission prophesied thirty years earlier in his poem *Science*, with its promise of "Fair Science" softening "with reforming Hand/ The native rudeness of a barbarous Land."

There still remained the rudeness of the newspaper press that, while making it perilous, had also made his mission possible. Before he died, Hopkinson had managed to tame the rudeness of at least his own newspaper writings, subduing them with a "reforming Hand" to a uniform gentility. In his obituary, Rush would have placed him with the great satiric spirits of the Western World—Swift, Rabelais, and Lucian, all of whom he imitated and sometimes well. But the next year in the *Universal Asylum* a reviewer of the posthumous *Miscellaneous Essays* complained that the satires were so personal and topical that they damaged the whole collection (8:110). The irony was that Hopkinson had already twice tried to make them more universal, once sometime before the close of 1782, in a two-volume notebook now at the Huntington Library and, sometime later, in five notebooks which are now at the Library of the American Philosophical Society. Those revisions removed his work even farther from the company of Swift, Rabelais, and Lucian and placed it closer to that of Addison and Steele, a company more proper for a state and then a federal judge, perhaps, but hardly in keeping with the Hopkinson his contemporaries once knew.

One glaring instance of the kind of revision he made is the omission of the entire "Preface" to *A Pretty Story* with its monolog by the madcap "Peter Grievous" teasing his readers; e.g., "Or, if you like not this, you may suppose that the following Sheets were found in the Cabinet of some deceased Gentleman; or that they were dug out of an ancient Ruins, or discovered in a . . . Hail Storm. In short you may suppose just what you please." This is the raucous tone of a man speaking to men—dramatic, colloquial, improvisational, a tone familiar to his contemporary readers from the popular *Tristram Shandy* and thus rousing their expectations of a comical turn. But the omission strips this antic voice from the original narrative and leaves it a more serious antique allegory of chiefly antiquarian charm.

Just as deplorable were those revisions that heightened the style while sacrificing the sense, as in this sample from the second chapter of *A Pretty Story*, which at first read:

> After some Time, however, by Dint of indefatigable Perseverance, they found themselves comfortably settled in this new Farm; and had the delightful Prospect of vast Tracts of Land waving with luxuriant Harvests, and perfuming the Air with delicious Fruits, which before had been a dreary Wilderness, unfit for the Habitation of Men.

In the notebooks of 1782 the passage is substantially the same except for added emphasis on the contrast between what the land was before and after the colonists came: ". . . with delicious Fruits where at their first Coming nothing saluted the Eye but a dreary & unmeasurable Wilderness." But in the later notebook, used as copy text for the *Miscellaneous Essays*, the paragraph is radically concise:

> After some Time, however, by their indefatigable Perseverance, they found themselves comfortably settled, & had the delightful Prospect of Fields waving with luxuriant Harvests & Orchards glowing with the Fruits of their Labour.

Printers of the *Miscellaneous Essays* discarded Hopkinson's practice of capitalizing nouns and also touched up his punctuation to remove the ambiguity that had the fields waving with luxurious orchards. Otherwise, this is the way the passage appeared in its final version (1:71). The revision does make it more concise and coherent, and does make the images more precise, since orchards at harvest time would glow rather than perfume the air. But the paragraph is so refined that it loses its function of contrasting the colorful fields with the dreary wilderness.

Revisions of this kind are so pervasive that they make it seem as though Hopkinson had worked through everything he had written, trying to raise it all to one uniform standard of melodious style. He had provided negative and positive samples of this standard in an oration to University students in 1785; first, positive:

> Some have a happy talent of expression, whereby they compensate the want of sentiment, by the melody of their style; their language, ever flowing like a wave of the sea, and their periods closing in such musical cadence, that the ear is fascinated by the magic of sound, and the mind lulled in a pleasing repose.

For contrast, he gave this negative example, "as offensive to the ear as the sharpening of a saw":

> Others, without giving to grammar rules offence, shall arrange so unskillfully their words, breaking, as it were, and interrupting the sense, or rather nonsense, they mean to inculcate, by frequent (and oft-times unnecessary) parenthesis, that the ear stumbles through the rugged paragraph, as the feet

> would stumble in scrambling through a street, when the pavement had been broken up, over bricks, stones, and posts, mixed together confusedly. (*Miscellaneous Essays,* 2:39)

It did not seem to matter whether this rough style was appropriate in its place. He polished it all, consistently transforming lively, disjointed speech patterns into the coherent, literary style that lulls the mind "in a pleasing repose."

In doing so, he violated the nature of such essays as "Consolation for the Old Bachelor," that pretends to be the monologue of "a tradesman in this city," given to such locutions as, "We were all tumbled hickledy-pickledy into the dirt." Speaking of stopping at Trenton to have lunch, he says in the original:

> Here we dined—my wife found fault with every thing; ate a very hearty dinner—declaring all the time there was nothing fit to eat. Miss *Jenny* crying out with the tooth-ach, her mother making sad lamentations—all my fault, because I did not make the glazier replace a broken pane of glass in her chamber window—

The revision makes him sound almost like Sir Roger de Coverley:

> Here we dined. My wife found fault with every thing; and whilst she disposed of what I thought a tolerable hearty meal, declared there was nothing fit to eat. Matters, however, would have gone on pretty well, but Miss *Jenny* began to cry with the tooth-ach—sad lamentations over Miss *Jenny*—all my fault, because I had not made the glazier replace a broken pane in her chamber window. (1:24)

The revision makes the passage more melodious and gives it tighter coherence, but also sacrifices psychological accuracy—since the point of the narrative is to illustrate the hubbub and confusion reflected in the style of the original version. In other words, the style of the original had been an image of what it was talking about.

This kind of violence is done even to a dramatic monologue such as "Nitidia's Answer," published originally in the *Columbian* while Hopkinson served as editor: "He had spilt a quantity of vitriol, and burnt a great hole in my carpet" becomes "He had spilt a quantity of vitriol upon my carpet, and burned a hole in it" (2:164); "My carpet. . . was destined to be most shamefully dishonoured in the afternoon, by a deluge of nasty tobacco juice—Gentlemen smoakers love segars better than carpets" becomes "My carpet . . . was destined to be shamefully dishonoured in the afternoon by a deluge of filthy tobacco juice—Gentlemen smokers and chewers, love segars and pigtail better than carpets" (2:167) where psychological accuracy is once again shamefully dishonored in the cause of logical coherence and melodious style.

The cumulative effect of such revisions drains these humorous essays of the lively, colloquial, sometimes vulgar qualities that made them seem to spring from the circumstances that first excited them. By sacrificing that air of improvisation and spontaneity, Hopkinson achieved a higher style but he violated the integrity of the essays themselves. He tried to raise the language to the level of the essays of Addison and Steele, yet only about a third of his own essays were the kind they had written—the "dream" allegories, some of the character sketches, and the letters from "foreigners" among the earlier works. The large majority, early and late, were patterned rather after Swift or Lucian or Franklin, with their self-deluded narrators and wily "projectors" reveling in ironic, nonsequential, often absurd yet subtly persuasive discourse, and relying upon psychological as opposed to logical coherence. The logical coherence that Hopkinson later imposed upon them was as inappropriate for them as scatology was for a judge of the state or federal courts.

Knowing his work in earlier versions, his contemporaries saw Hopkinson as the "inimitable master of wit and humor" (*Packet,* 12 February 1787). But even in 1960, in some cases reading the revisions alone, so discriminating a critic as Bruce Granger could see him as "the foremost essayist of the Revolution."[13] This could

13. *Political Satire in the American Revolution* (Ithaca, 1960), p. 23.

be owing to Hopkinson's having relied for effect less on style than on character and situation and idea. Put another way, if we say humor is the perception of the ridiculous, and wit is its expression, then Hopkinson focused on humor.

These humorous essays convey a charm in distinct contrast with the angry, Juvenalian satires produced by such now more familiar contemporaries as Philip Freneau, and with the coolly dispassionate satires by Franklin such as the "Edict of the King of Prussia." Hopkinson's were more like Franklin's bagatelles, more playful than critical, as though illustrating a principle he lightly tossed off in the essay called "Common Amusements": "The miseries, misfortunes, and sufferings of our fellow creatures can never be proper subjects of ridicule; but the passions, follies, and excentricities of mankind are surely lawful occasions of laughter." For him, both the source and end of humor lay in the lively interplay of words, images, feelings, and ideas. The mark of the true humorist is his "amazing facility in associating ludicrous ideas to the most ordinary and seemingly the most barren incidents of life."

In some of the purely playful essays he could exploit ambiguity of language for its own sake, as in Nitidia's puns and "switches" —where we are led to expect the sentence to end one way but find it switching to another: "When one is about a thorough cleaning—the first dirty thing to be removed is one's husband." More often, he focused on the ambiguity of language as a common root of "the passions, follies, and excentricities" of men who mistake the letter of language for its meaning. Thus, the catalog of Rivington's merchandise lets irony run riot, and "The Art of Paper War" tortures the medium to fit the message.

But at its best, Hopkinson's humor focuses on the incongruous images and absurd ideas abounding in everyday life. Typically his essays exploit familiar objects in new relations, as the giant pendulum or wooden horse show up Congressional folly. The more imaginative essays still are those which, like Swift's, set up a spokesman for some outrageous argument and have him maintain it in the face of common sense or common humanity—letting him demonstrate its absurdity out of his own mouth, unconsciously revealing himself to be a fool or moral monster. Thus Admiral Collier and General Tryon declare solemnly that the only reason they have set fire to people's homes is to provide light for reading proclamations by night, and Rivington swears that the reason he printed so many monstrous lies was his conviction that only the British would have been stupid enough to believe them.

With perceptions of this order and the skills to convey them, Hopkinson could have succeeded Franklin as the nation's foremost satirist, and become the American Swift or Rabelais or Lucian, for he shared their moral concerns. In filibustering before the assembly, the wooden post speaks of man's pride in being a rational creature: "When nature gave one man the power to *reason*, she gave another the power to *laugh* at him." Man is ridiculous when he uses reason to deceive himself; contemptible when he uses reason to deceive others: "To over-reach, deceive, ruin and destroy . . . to conceal or embarrass truth, to establish falshood, to lead the blind out of his way and the lame into a ditch." Into the mouth of his madman in "The New Roof" Hopkinson puts the moralist's paradox: "Oh God! what a monster is man!—A being possessed of knowledge, reason, judgment and an immortal soul —what a monster is man!" Still he wrote less as a moralist than as a satirist, and less as a satirist than a humorist who preferred to laugh at moral ambiguities rather than lament what man has made of man.

He called the best of his later essays "Some Thoughts on the Diseases of the Mind; with a Scheme for purging the Moral Faculties," and there proposed that "an intimate connection" between the disorders of the body and the soul caused most of man's miseries. An insatiable rage for slander and abuse, often the subject of earlier essays, is here diagnosed as a natural "disease peculiar to free governments," requiring a free press as a vent "for the morbid minds of the people to get rid of their impurities, and the opportunity of keeping up a free circulation of ideas, so necessary to the mental health of man." As a public health measure, then, he proposes that two newspapers—one weekly, one daily—be set aside exclusively for venting slander and abuse, leaving other papers free to circulate ideas, information, and entertainment: "All the filth in the city would be carried off by the commissioned papers," and the time would come when it would be "as shocking to good manners for a man to vent his spleen in one of the public *news* papers . . . as it would be to commit an indecent evacuation in a private parlour, or a public assembly." He could easily have treated the problem of an irresponsible press as a serious moral issue, yet typically preferred to treat it as another instance of man's "passions, follies, and excentricities"—the province of the true humorist that he chose, out of diffidence or conviction, to be.

In trying to convey this comic spirit, I have felt that reproducing Hopkinson's texts exactly as they first appeared would impose obstacles for modern readers unfamiliar with such older printing conventions as the long s or the use of different kinds of types to show varying degrees of emphasis. For that reason, I have not retained even the practice of using capital letters for all nouns, except in *A Pretty Story*, where it contributes to comic effect. Otherwise, such conventions are modernized and typographical errors silently corrected, except when they, too, contribute to an effect that might have been intentional. Fortunately we can check such intentions against the manuscripts at the Huntington Library and at the Library of the American Philosophical Society.

These libraries, along with the Pennsylvania Historical Society, the Library Company of Philadelphia, and the University of Pennsylvania, have also provided material for the texts and commentary. The notes are based so far as possible on contemporary sources, supplemented by the exhaustive detail gathered by the late George Hastings for his *Life and Works of Francis Hopkinson* (1926) and later articles in the *Dictionary of American Biography* (DAB) and *American Literature* (AL). They have also profited from the work of other specialists—Dixon Wecter, Lewis Leary, Bruce Granger, and contributors to the *William and Mary Quarterly* (WMQ) and the *Pennsylvania Magazine of History and Biography* (PMHB). For the most part, however, both notes and commentary derive directly from the newspapers and periodicals that first carried Hopkinson's work—for my intent has been to clarify allusions not only as they existed in fact but as they seemed to exist to Hopkinson and his first readers.

This edition has thus been made possible by the gracious permission of the Huntington Library, the Pennsylvania Historical Society, the Library Company of Philadelphia, and the University of Pennsylvania to reproduce material in their holdings. The staff of the Huntington Library has comforted me with blessings of all kinds, while Teresa Bertucci served tirelessly in helping to compile the texts, as did Elisabeth Zall in this and other ways.

San Marino, 1974 PMZ

# *A PRETTY STORY* (1774)

On 15 August 1774, the *Pennsylvania Packet* advertised a slight, twenty-nine-page pamphlet with the teasing title, "*A Pretty Story*, Written in the Year of our Lord 2774, by Peter Grievous, Esq; A. B. C. D. E." This was Hopkinson's allegory about the deterioration in Anglo-American relations that led to the demand for a continental congress. Since June, various colonial conventions and assemblies had been issuing "resolves" to the same effect, and a congress had indeed been scheduled for Philadelphia in September. *A Pretty Story* focused on the constitutional issues to be faced then, and also outlined the platform voters ought to consider when choosing delegates. Bluntly, it was radical propaganda.

The allegory is about a noble farmer's sons who, having built a profitable plantation in a distant land, now find their prosperity threatened by the insatiable greed of their wicked stepmother and her wily lover. The narrative chronicles the family ties from the signing of Magna Charta down to July 1774 when Parliament blockaded Boston Port. Its point is to prove that in closing the Port, as in other acts of the past ten years, Parliament (the stepmother) and the prime minister (her lover) had acted unconstitutionally, violating common-law rights of the colonists who were, after all, British subjects by birthright.

The constitutional issue had been heating since 1766 when Parliament, in repealing the Stamp Act, passed a Declaratory Act declaring its right to legislate for the colonies "in all cases whatsoever." The colonies accepted this until they realized Parliament was talking about internal taxation. In 1767 came a new set of duties on imports to cover costs of defense against the French and Indians. The colonists again resisted, as they had resisted the Stamp Act, with nonimportation agreements, until three years later the duties were repealed—all except a tax on tea. Lord North, the prime minister, insisted that the tax on tea remain as a symbol of the right asserted in the Declaratory Act. Boston resisted even that, and Parliament reacted with the Intolerable Acts—closing Boston Port and revoking self-government. The next move belonged to the colonies, and Hopkinson's tale stops on this note of suspense, leaving no doubt about the need for a decisive declaration of economic independence at least.

Ever since the Intolerable Acts had been announced in the spring, the press had tried to ignite widespread support first for the relief of Boston and then for a congress. But there was hardly a consensus. Radicals had been urging any means necessary to achieve economic freedom. Conservatives were begging for moderation, asking that demands be limited to restoring the status the colonies enjoyed before the Stamp Act. Reactionaries insisted on conciliating the mother country at any cost. The undecided majority thus became the target of propaganda from three sides. Political essays squeezed advertisements into small corners of such popular newspapers as the *Packet,* and most of those essays would then be published as pamphlets. It would not be surprising, in fact, if Hopkinson had written his story for the *Packet* only to find no room therein and instead published it as a pamphlet directly. In any case, it proved popular enough to warrant two editions in Philadelphia and a reprint in Wilmington, Delaware, before the year was out.

Its popularity was deserved, for, though it said what others had been saying, *A Pretty Story* offered comic relief in a dismal swamp of didactic "resolves," exhortatory pamphlets, and tediously abstract political essays. Peter Grievous bounced onto the scene, a busy hack with no ax to grind, utterly unconscious of and unconcerned about the implications of the tale he told, full of sound and fury signifying revolution. His readers readily recognized the allegorical figures and allusions: The Old Nobleman was the king; his Wife, called "Mother-in-law" (i.e. stepmother), was Parliament; the Steward was the prime minister; Jack was Boston; the gruel was tea; the padlock on Jack's gate, the Boston Port Act; and so on. For the otherwise uninitiated, there was a motto after Plutarch, *Veluti in Speculo,* announcing that the book was a mirror of real life. But most readers were familiar with this kind of story from the popular works of Swift like *A Tale of a Tub,* with its hero named Jack, and from Arbuthnot's *History of John Bull* (available in Swift's *Miscellanies*), where the king of England is an Old Gentleman whose Wife is debauched by his Steward.

More recently, Franklin had used similar Swiftian allegories and fables to attack Parliament in the British newspapers. In a letter of early 1774, he assumed the mask of a London tradesman who suffered grievously from declining commerce with the colonies: "Will honest *John Bull,* the Farmer, be long satisfied with Servants, that before his

Face attempt to kill his *Plow Horses?*"[1] During the winter, the *Packet* had run his "Edict of the King of Prussia," satirizing restrictions on colonial manufacture—satirized also in *A Pretty Story*—with the same emphasis on "the better peopling" of the new land. As recently as the first week of August, a fortnight before Hopkinson's story appeared, the *Packet* had run Franklin's "Rules by which a Great Empire may be Reduced to a Small One," setting the pattern for Hopkinson's irony and exciting readers' imaginations as though preparing their minds for *A Pretty Story*.

## PREFACE

A book without a Preface is like a Face without a Nose. Let the other Features be ever so agreeable and well proportioned, it is looked on with Detestation and Horror if this material Ornament be wanting.

Or rather, a Book is like a House: The grand Portico is the Dedication; the flagged Pavement is an humble Address to the Reader, in Order to pave the Way for a kind Reception of the Work; the Front Door with its fluted Pillars, Pediment, Trigliffs and Modillons are the Title Page with its Motto, Author's Name and Titles, Date of the Year, &c. The Entry is the Preface (oftentimes of a tedious Length) and the several Apartments and Closets are the Chapters and Sections of the Work itself.

As I am but a clumsy Carpenter at best, I shall not attempt to decorate my little Cottage with any *out of Door* Ornaments; but as it would be inconvenient and uncomfortable to have my Front Door open immediately into the Apartments of my House, I have made this Preface by Way of Entry.

And now, gentle Reader, if you should think my Entry too plain and simple you may set your Imagination to work, and furnish it with a grand Staircase, with Cornices, Stucco and Paintings. That

1. Benjamin Franklin, *Writings of Benjamin Franklin*, ed. A. H. Smyth, (New York, 1906) 6:218.

is, you may suppose that I entered very unwillingly upon this Work, being compelled to it by a Chain of unforeseen Circumstances: That it was written in the Midst of a great Hurry of other Business, and under particular Disadvantages of Time and Place, and that it was only intended for the Inspection of a few Friends, without any Expectations of ever seeing it in the Press.

You may, kind Reader, go on to suppose that when my Friends perused my Work, they were struck with the Energy of my Genius, and insisted that the Public ought not to be deprived of such a Fund of Amusement and Improvement through my obstinate Modesty; and that after many Solicitations and powerful Persuasions I had been prevailed upon to bless Mankind with the Fruits of my Labour.

Or, if you like not this, you may suppose that the following Sheets were found in the Cabinet of some deceased Gentleman; or that they were dug out of an ancient Ruins, or discovered in a Hermit's Cave, or dropped from the Clouds in a Hail Storm. In short you may suppose just what you please. And when, by the Help of Imagination, you have seasoned the Preface to your Palate, you may turn over this Leaf, and feast upon the Body of the Work itself.

## CHAPTER I

Once upon a Time, a great While ago, there lived a certain Nobleman, who had long possessed a very valuable Farm, and had a great Number of Children and Grandchildren.

Besides the annual Profits of his Land, which were very considerable, he kept a large Shop of Goods; and being very successful in Trade, he became, in Process of Time, exceeding rich and powerful; insomuch that all his Neighbours feared and respected him.

With Respect to the Management of his Family, it was thought he had adopted the most perfect Mode that could be devised, for he had been at the Pains to examine the Œconomy of all his Neighbours, and had selected from their Plans all such Parts as appeared to be equitable and beneficial, and omitted those which from Experience were found to be inconvenient. Or rather, by blending their several Constitutions together he had so ingeniously counterbalanced the Evils of one Mode of Government with the Benefits of another, that the Advantages were richly enjoyed, and the Inconveniencies scarcely felt. In short, his Family was thought to be the best ordered of any in his Neighbourhood.

He never exercised any undue Authority over his Children or Servants; neither indeed could he oppress them if he was so disposed; for it was particularly covenanted in his Marriage Articles that he should not at any Time impose any Tasks or Hardships whatever upon his Children without the free Consent of his Wife.

Now the Custom in his Family was this, that at the End of every seven Years his Marriage became of Course null and void;[2] at which Time his Children and Grandchildren met together and chose another Wife for him, whom the old Gentleman was

---

2. The Septennial Act (1716) required Parliamentary elections at least every seven years.

obliged to marry under the same Articles and Restrictions as before. If his late Wife had conducted herself, during her seven Year's Marriage, with Mildness, Discretion and Integrity, she was re-elected; if otherwise, deposed: By which Means the Children had always a great Interest in their Mother in Law; and through her, a reasonable Check upon their Father's Temper. For besides that he could do nothing material respecting his Children without her Approbation, she was sole Mistress of the Purse Strings; and gave him out, from Time to Time, such Sums of Money as she thought necessary for the Expences of his Family.

Being one Day in a very extraordinary good Humour, he gave his Children a Writing under his Hand and Seal, by which he released them from many Badges of Dependance, and confirmed to them several very important Privileges. The chief were the two following, viz. that none of his Children should be punished for any Offence, or supposed Offence, until his Brethren had first declared him worthy of such Punishment; and secondly, he gave fresh Assurances that he would impose no Hardships upon them without the Consent of their Mother in Law.

This Writing, on Account of its singular Importance, was called *The Great Paper*. After it was executed with the utmost Solemnity, he caused his Chaplain to publish a dire *Anathema* against all who should attempt to violate the Articles of the *Great Paper*, in the Words following.

"In the Name of the *Father, Son* and *Holy Ghost*, AMEN![3] Whereas our Lord and Master, to the Honour of God and for the common Profit of this Farm hath granted, for him and his Heirs forever, these Articles above written: I, his Chaplain and spiritual Pastor of all this Farm, do admonish the People of the Farm *Once, Twice,* and *Thrice:* Because that Shortness will not suffer so much Delay as to give Knowledge to the People of these Presents in Writing; I therefore enjoyn all Persons, of what Estate soever they be, that they and every of them, as much as in them

3. *This is a true and genuine Denunciation copied from the Archives of the Family.* [Hopkinson's note.] In Latin, this "Sentencia lata super Cartas" was available in Owen Ruffhead, ed., *Statutes at Large* (London, 1763), 1:21.

is, shall uphold and maintain these Articles granted by our Lord and Master in all Points. And all those that in any Point do resist, or break, or in any Manner hereafter procure, counsel or any Ways assent to resist or break these Ordinances, or go about it by Word or Deed, openly or privately, by any Manner of Pretence or Colour: I the aforesaid Chaplain, by my Authority, do *excommunicate* and *accurse*, and from the Body of our Lord *Jesus Christ*, and from all the *Company of Heaven*, and from all the *Sacraments* of holy Church do *sequester* and *exclude*."

## CHAPTER II

Now it came to pass that this Nobleman had, by some Means or other, obtained a Right to an immense Tract of wild uncultivated Country at a vast Distance from his Mansion House. But he set little Store by this Acquisition, as it yielded him no Profit; nor was it likely to do so, being not only difficult of Access on Account of the [Dis]tance, but was also overrun with innumerable wild Beasts very fierce and savage; so that it would be extremely dangerous to attempt taking Possession of it.

In Process of Time, however, some of his Children, more stout and enterprising than the rest, requested Leave of their Father to go and settle on this distant Tract of Land. Leave was readily obtained; but before they set out certain Agreements were stipulated between them—the principal were—The old Gentleman, on his Part, engaged to protect and defend the Adventurers in their new Settlements; to assist them in chacing away the wild Beasts, and to extend to them all the Benefits of the Government under which they were born: Assuring them that although they should be removed so far from his Presence they should nevertheless be considered as the Children of his Family, and treated accordingly. At the same Time he gave each of them a Bond for the faithful Performance of these Promises; in which, among other Things, it was covenanted that they should, each of them in their several Families, have a Liberty of making such Rules and Regulations for their own good Government as they should find convenient;

provided these Rules and Regulations should not contradict or be inconsistent with the general standing Orders established in his Farm.

In return for these Favours he insisted that they, on their Parts, should at all Times acknowledge him to be their Father; that they should not deal with their Neighbours without his Leave, but send to his Shop only for such Merchandize as they should want. But in Order to enable them to pay for such Goods as they should purchase, they were permitted to sell the Produce of their Lands to certain of his Neighbours.

These Preliminaries being duly adjusted, our Adventurers bid Adieu to the Comforts and Conveniencies of their Father's House, and set off on their Journey—Many and great were the Difficulties they encountered on their Way: but many more and much greater had they to combat on their Arrival in the new Country. Here they found Nothing but wild Nature. Mountains over-grown with inaccessible Foliage, and Plains steeped in stagnated Waters. Their Ears are no longer attentive to the repeated Strokes of industrious Labour and the busy Hum of Men, instead of these, the roaring Tempest and incessant Howlings of Beasts of Prey fill their Minds with Ho[r]ror and Dismay. The needful Comforts of Life are no longer in their Power—no friendly Roof to shelter them from inclement Skies; no Fortress to protect them from surrounding Dangers. Unaccustomed as they were to Hardships like these, some were cut off by Sickness and Disease, and others snatched away by the Hands of Barbarity. They began however, with great Perseverance, to clear the Land of encumbering Rubbish, and the Woods resound with the Strokes of Labour; they drain the Waters from the sedged Morass, and pour the Sun Beams on the reeking Soil; they are forced to exercise all the Powers of Industry and Œconomy for bare Subsistence, and like their first Parent, when driven from Paradise, to earn their Bread with the Sweat of their Brows. In this Work they were frequently interrupted by the Incursions of the wild Beasts, against whom they defended themselves with heroic Prowess and Magnanimity.

After some Time, however, by Dint of indefatigable Perseverance, they found themselves comfortably settled in this new Farm; and had the delightful Prospect of vast Tracts of Land waving with luxuriant Harvests, and perfuming the Air with delicious Fruits, which before had been a dreary Wilderness, unfit for the Habitation of Men.

In the mean Time they kept up a constant Correspondence with their Father's Family, and at a great Expence provided Waggons, Horses and Drivers to bring from his Shop such Goods and Merchandize as they wanted, for which they paid out of the Produce of their Lands.

## CHAPTER III

Now the new Settlers had adopted a Mode of Government in their several Families similar to that their Father had established in the old Farm; in taking a new Wife at the End of certain Periods of Time; which Wife was chosen for them by their Children, and without whose Consent they could do nothing material in the Conduct of their Affairs. Under these Circumstances they thrived exceedingly, and became very numerous; living in great Harmony amongst themselves, and in constitutional Obedience to their Father and his Wife.

Notwithstanding their successful Progress, however, they were frequently annoyed by the wild Beasts, which were not yet expelled the Country; and were moreover troubled by some of their Neighbours who wanted to drive them off the Land, and take Possession of it themselves.

To assist them in these Difficulties, and protect them from Danger, the old Nobleman sent over several of his Servants, who with the Help of the new Settlers drove away their Enemies. But then he required that they should reimburse him for the Expence and Trouble he was at in their Behalf; this they did with great Cheerfulness, by applying from Time to Time to their respective Wives, who always commanded their Cash.

Thus did Matters go on for a considerable Time, to their mutual Happiness and Benefit. But now the Nobleman's Wife began to cast an avaricious Eye upon the new Settlers; saying to herself, if by the natural Consequence of their Intercourse with us my Wealth and Power are so much increased, how much more would they accumulate if I can persuade them that all they have belonged to us, and therefore I may at any Time demand from them such Part of their Earnings as I please. At the same Time she was fully sensible of the Promises and Agreements her Husband had made when they left the old Farm, and of the Tenor and Purport of the *Great Paper*. She therefore thought it necessary to proceed with great Caution and Art, and endeavoured to gain her Point by imperceptible Steps.

In Order to this, she first issued an Edict setting forth, That whereas the Tailors of her Family were greatly injured by the People of the new Farm, inasmuch as they presumed to make their own Clothes whereby the said Tailors were deprived of the Benefit of their Custom; it was therefore ordained that for the future the new Settlers should not be permitted to have amongst them any Shears or Scissars larger than a certain fixed size.[4] In Consequence of this, our Adventurers were compelled to have their Clothes made by their Father's Tailors: But out of Regard to the old Gentleman, they patiently submitted to this Grievance.

Encouraged by this Success, she proceeded in her Plan. Observing that the new Settlers were very fond of a particular Kind of Cyder which they purchased of a Neighbour, who was in Friendship with their Father (the Apples proper for making this Cyder not growing on their own Farm) she published another Edict, obliging them to pay her a certain Stipend for every Barrel of Cyder used in their Families![5] To this likewise they submitted: Not yet seeing the Scope of her Designs against them.

After this Manner she proceeded, imposing Taxes upon them on various Pretences, and receiving the Fruits of their Industry

---

4. To protect English industry, Americans were forbidden to export hats and woolens (1732) or expand iron manufacture (1750).
5. Wines imported directly from Madeira, the Azores and the Canary Islands were heavily taxed (1764).

with both Hands. Moreover she persuaded her Husband to send amongst them from Time to Time a Number of the most lazy and useless of his Servants, under the specious Pretext of defending them in their Settlements,[6] and of assisting to destroy the wild Beasts; but in Fact to rid his own House of their Company, not having Employment for them; and at the same Time to be a Watch and a Check upon the People of the new Farm.

It was likewise ordered that these Protectors, as they were called, should be supplied with Bread and Butter cut in a particular Form: But the Head of one of the Families refused to comply with this Order.[7] He engaged to give the Guests, thus forced upon him, Bread and Butter sufficient; but insisted that his Wife should have the Liberty of cutting it in what Shape she pleased.

This put the old Nobleman into a violent Passion, insomuch that he had his Son's Wife put into Gaol for presuming to cut her Loaf otherwise than as had been directed.

## CHAPTER IV

As the old Gentleman advanced in Years he began to neglect the Affairs of his Family, leaving them chiefly to the Management of his Steward. Now the Steward had debauched his Wife, and by that Means gained an entire Ascendency over her. She no longer deliberated what would most benefit either the old Farm or the new; but said and did whatever the Steward pleased. Nay so much was she influenced by him that she could neither utter *Ay* or *No* but as he directed. For he had cunningly persuaded her that it was very fashionable for Women to wear Padlocks on their Lips, and that he was sure they would become her exceed-

---

6. At the close of the French-Indian War (1763), seventeen regiments were to remain in America, supported after the second year by local taxes.
7. Annual Mutiny, or Quartering, Acts specified the goods and services to be furnished by each colony. In 1766, New York refused to supply salt, vinegar, cider, and beer. The next year, Parliament suspended the assembly's powers until New York complied.

ingly. He therefore fastened a Padlock to each Corner of her Mouth; when the one was open, she could only say *Ay;* and when the other was loosed, could only cry *No.* He took Care to keep the Keys of these Locks himself; so that her Will became entirely subject to his Power.

Now the old Lady and the Steward had set themselves against the People of the new Farm; and began to devise Ways and Means to impoverish and distress them.

They prevailed on the Nobleman to sign an Edict against the new Settlers, in which it was declared that it was their Duty as Children to pay something towards the supplying their Father's Table with Provisions, and to the supporting the Dignity of his Family; for that Purpose it was ordained that all their Spoons, Knives and Forks, Plates and Porringers, should be marked with a certain Mark, by Officers appointed for that End;[8] for which marking they were to pay a certain Stipend: And that they should not, under severe Penalties, presume to make use of any Spoon, Knife or Fork, Plate or Porringer, before it had been so marked, and the said Stipend paid to the Officer.

The Inhabitants of the new Farm began to see that their Father's Affections were alienated from them; and that their Mother was but a base Mother in Law debauched by their Enemy the Steward. They were thrown into great Confusion and Distress. They wrote the most supplicating Letters to the old Gentleman, in which they acknowledged him to be their Father in Terms of the greatest Respect and Affection—they recounted to him the Hardships and Difficulties they had suffered in settling his new Farm; and pointed out the great Addition of Wealth and Power his Family had acquired by the Improvement of that Wilderness; and showed him that all the Fruits of their Labours must in the natural Course of Things unite, in the long Run, in his Money Box. They also, in humble Terms, reminded him of his Promises and Engagements on their leaving Home, and of the Bonds he

8. Under the Stamp Act (1765), local agents appointed by the Crown sold the stamps required for all legal and commercial papers, including newspapers and pamphlets.

had given them; of the Solemnity and Importance of the *Great Paper* with the Curse annexed. They acknowledged that he ought to be reimbursed the Expences he was at on their Account, and that it was their Duty to assist in supporting the Dignity of his Family. All this they declared they were ready and willing to do; but requested that they might do it agreeable to the Purport of the *Great Paper,* by applying to their several Wives for the Keys of their Money Boxes and furnishing him from thence; and not be subject to the Tyranny and Caprice of an avaricious Mother in Law, whom they had never chosen, and of a Steward who was their declared Enemy.

Some of these Letters were intercepted by the Steward; others were delivered to the old Gentleman, who was at the same Time persuaded to take no Notice of them;[9] but, on the Contrary, to insist the more strenuously upon the Right his Wife claimed of marking their Spoons, Knives and Forks, Plates and Porringers.

The new Settlers observing how Matters were conducted in their Father's Family became exceedingly distressed and mortified. They met together and agreed one and all that they would no longer submit to the arbitrary Impositions of their Mother in Law, and their Enemy the Steward.[10] They determined to pay no Manner of Regard to the new Decree, considering it as a Violation of the *Great Paper.* But to go on and eat their Broth and Pudding as usual. The Cooks also and Butlers served up their Spoons, Knives and Forks, Plates and Porringers without having them marked by the new Officers.

The Nobleman at length thought fit to reverse the Order which

---

9. An article in the *Pennsylvania Packet* for 6 June 1774 reminded readers ("You remember . . ."), "The petitions of our assemblies" against the Stamp Act, "asserting our rights, and supplicating a respect for them, were treated with contempt." In 1765, Franklin received reports that Philadelphians were incensed by rumors of the Privy Council rejecting "the Humble Petition of their Representatives without even a Hearing" and preventing their reaching the king (*Writings*, ed. Smyth, 4:365).
10. The Stamp Act Congress (1765) had resolved that Parliament had no constitutional right to tax the colonies without their consent. Threats and violence forced stamp agents to resign, and nonimportation agreements effectively boycotted English goods.

*Funeral of the Stamp Tax (18 March 1766)*

*Led by George Grenville, father of the Stamp Tax, anti-American politicians bear their favorite child, merely twelve months old, to the family vault.*

---

had been made respecting the Spoons, Knives and Forks, Plates and Porringers of the new Settlers. But he did this with a very ill Grace: For he, at the same Time avowed and declared that he and his Wife had a Right to mark all their Furniture, if they pleased, from the Silver Tankard down to the very Chamber Pots:[11] That as he was their Father he had an absolute Controul over them, and that their Liberties, Lives and Properties were at

11. Immediately upon repealing the Stamp Act (1766), Parliament passed the Declaratory Act asserting the right to legislate for the colonies without their consent "in all cases whatsoever."

the entire Disposal of him and his Wife: That it was not fit that he who was allowed to be *Omnipresent, Immortal,* and *incapable of Error,* should be confined by the Shackles of the *Great Paper;* or obliged to fulfil the Bonds he had given them, which he averred he had a Right to cancel whenever he pleased.

His Wife also became intoxicated with Vanity. The Steward had told her that she was an *omnipotent* Goddess, and ought to be worshipped as such: That it was the Height of Impudence and Disobedience in the new Settlers to dispute her Authority, which, with Respect to them, was unlimited: That as they had removed from their Father's Family, they had forfeited all Pretensions to be considered as his Children, and lost the Privileges of the *Great Paper:* That, therefore, she might look on them only as Tenants at Will upon her Husband's Farm, and exact from them what Rent she pleased.

All this was perfectly agreeable to Madam, who admitted this new Doctrine in its full Sense.

The People of the new Farm however took little Notice of these pompous Declarations. They were glad the marking Decree was reversed, and were in Hopes that Things would gradually settle into their former Channel.

## CHAPTER V

In the mean Time the new Settlers increased exceedingly, and as they increased, their Dealings at their Father's Shop were proportionally enlarged.

It is true they suffered some Inconveniencies from the Protectors that had been sent amongst them, who became very troublesome in their Houses: They seduced their Daughters; introduced Riot and Intemperance into their Families, and derided and insulted the Orders and Regulations they had made for their own good Government. Moreover the old Nobleman had sent amongst them a great Number of Thieves, Ravishers and Murderers, who did a great deal of Mischief by practising those Crimes for which they had been banished the old Farm. But they bore these Grievances with as much Patience as could be expected; not choosing to trouble their aged Father with Complaints, unless in Cases of important Necessity.

Now the Steward continued to hate the new Settlers with exceeding great Hatred, and determined to renew his Attack upon their Peace and Happiness. He artfully insinuated to the old Gentleman and his foolish Wife, that it was very mean and unbecoming in them to receive the Contributions of the People of the new Farm, towards supporting the Dignity of his Family, through the Hands of their respective Wives: That upon this Footing it would be in their Power to refuse his Requisitions whenever they should be thought to be unreasonable, of which they would pretend to be Judges themselves; and that it was high Time they should be compelled to acknowledge his arbitrary Power, and his Wife's *Omnipotence*.

For this Purpose, another Decree was prepared and published, ordering that the new Settlers should pay a certain Stipend upon particular Goods, which they were not allowed to purchase any where but at their Father's Shop; and that this Stipend should not be deemed an Advance upon the original Price of the Goods, but be paid on their Arrival at the new Farm, for the express Purpose of supporting the Dignity of the old Gentleman's Family, and of defraying the Expences he affected to afford them.[12]

This new Decree gave our Adventurers the utmost Uneasiness. They saw that the Steward and their Mother in Law were determined to oppress and enslave them. They again met together and wrote to their Father, as before, the most humble and persuasive Letters;[13] but to little Purpose: A deaf Ear was turned to all their Remonstrances; and their dutiful Requests treated with Contempt.

Finding this moderate and decent Conduct brought them no Relief, they had Recourse to another Expedient. They bound

---

12. The Townshend Act (1767) levied duties on glass, lead for paint, pigment, tea, and paper expressly to defray "the charge of the administration of justice and the support of civil government."

13. In early 1768, Massachusetts and Virginia petitioned for repeal of the Townshend duties and asked other colonies to follow suit.

themselves in a solemn Engagement not to deal any more at their Father's Shop until this unconstitutional Decree should be reversed;[14] which they declared to be a Violation of the *Great Paper.*

This Agreement was so strictly adhered to, that in a few Months the Clerks and Apprentices in the old Gentleman's Shop began to make a sad Outcry. They declared that their Master's Trade was declining exceedingly, and that his Wife and Steward would, by their mischievious Machinations, ruin the whole Farm:[15] They forthwith sharpened their Pens and attacked the Steward, and even the old Lady herself with great Severity. Insomuch that it was thought proper to withdraw this Attempt likewise upon the Rights and Liberties of the new Settlers. One Part only of the new Decree remained unreversed—Viz. the Tax upon *Water Gruel.*

Now there were certain Men on the old Farm, who had obtained from the Nobleman an exclusive Right of selling *Water Gruel.* Vast Quantities of this *Gruel* were vended amongst the new Settlers; for it became very fashionable for them to use it in their Families in great Abundance. They did not however trouble themselves much about the Tax on *Water Gruel:* They were well pleased with the Reversal of the other Parts of the Decree, and considering *Gruel* as not absolutely necessary to the Comfort of Life, they were determined to endeavour to do without it, and by that Means avoid the remaining Effects of the new Decree.

The Steward found his Designs once more frustrated; but was not discouraged by this Disappointment. He formed another Scheme so artfully contrived that he thought himself sure of Success.[16] He sent for the Persons who had the sole Right of vending

---

14. Nonimportation agreements were revived, remaining in effect until March 1770 when the duties on all but tea were lifted.
15. A letter in the London *Public Advertiser* for 17 January 1769 complained that Townshend revenues amounted to £3500 annually, but losses from boycotts had already amounted to £7,250,000.
16. In 1773, when the East India Company petitioned to remove the tax on tea, Lord North refused, maintaining "the right of taxing Americans." But he did provide for refunding the English import duties the Company paid on tea reexported to America.

*Water Gruel,* and after reminding them of the Obligations they were under to the Nobleman and his Wife for their exclusive Privilege, he desired that they would send sundry Waggon Loads of *Gruel* to the new Farm, promising that the accustomed Duty which they paid for their exclusive Right should be taken off from all the *Gruel* they should send amongst the new Settlers: And that in Case their Cargoes should come to any Damage, he would take Care that the Loss should be repaired out of the old Gentleman's Coffers.

The *Gruel* Merchants readily consented to this Proposal, knowing that if their Cargoes were sold, they would reap considerable Profits; and if they failed, the Steward was to make good the Damage. On the other Hand the Steward concluded that the new Settlers could not resist purchasing the *Gruel* to which they had been so long accustomed; and if they did purchase it when subject to the Tax aforesaid, this would be an avowed Acknowledgment on their Parts that their Father and his Wife had a Right to break through the Tenor of the *Great Paper,* and to lay on them what Impositions they pleased, without the Consent of their respective Wives.

But the new Settlers were well aware of this Decoy. They saw clearly that the *Gruel* was not sent to accommodate, but to enslave them; and that if they suffered any Part of it to be sold amongst them, it would be deemed a Submission to the assumed *Omnipotence* of the *Great Madam.*

## CHAPTER VI

On the Arrival of the *Water Gruel,* the People of the new Farm were again thrown into great Alarms and Confusions. Some of them would not suffer the Waggons to be unloaded at all, but sent them immediately back to the *Gruel* Merchants: Others permitted the Waggons to unload, but would not touch the hateful Commodity; so that it lay neglected about their Roads and Highways until it grew sour and spoiled. But one of the new Settlers, whose Name was *Jack,* either from a keener Sense of the Injuries attempted against him, or from the Necessity of his Situation, which was such that he could not send back the *Gruel* because of a Number of Mercenaries whom his Father had stationed before his House to watch and be a Check upon his Conduct:[17] He, I say, being almost driven to Despair, fell to Work, and with great Zeal stove to Pieces the Casks of *Gruel,* which had been sent him, and utterly demolished the whole Cargoe.

These Proceedings were soon known at the old Farm. Great and terrible was the Uproar there. The old Gentleman fell into great Wrath, declaring that his absent Children meant to throw off all Dependence upon him, and to become altogether disobedient. His Wife also tore the Padlocks from her Lips, and raved and stormed like a Billingsgate. The Steward lost all Patience and Moderation, swearing most prophanely that he would leave no Stone unturned 'till he had *humbled the Settlers of the new Farm at his Feet,*[18] and caused their Father to trample on their Necks. Moreover the *Gruel* Merchants roared and bellowed for the Loss of their *Gruel;* and the Clerks and Apprentices were in the utmost Consternation lest the People of the new Farm should again agree to have no Dealings with their Father's Shop —Vengeance was immediately set on Foot, particularly against *Jack.* With him they determined to begin; hoping that by making an Example of him they should so terrify the other Families of the new Settlers, that they would all submit to the Designs of the Steward, and the *Omnipotence* of the old Lady.

A very large *Padlock* was, accordingly, prepared to be fastened upon *Jack's* great Gate;[19] the Key of which was to given to the old

---

17. In November 1767, a Board of Customs Commissioners in North America was established, based in Boston, inciting increasing hostility.
18. This echoes a notorious statement on Americans and America by Lord North during debates on repealing the Townshend duties, reprinted in the *Pennsylvania Packet* for 20 June 1774: "Now is the time to stand out—to *defy* them —to proceed in *earnest;* and that we will proceed with firmness and rigour— until SHE SHALL BE LAID AT OUR FEET."
19. The Boston Port Act (7 March 1774) said that after 1 June, no vessel might enter Boston Harbor and after 14 June none might leave. This was followed

Gentleman; who was not to open it again until he had paid for the *Gruel* he had spilt, and resigned all Claim to the Privileges of the *Great Paper:* Nor then neither unless he thought fit. Secondly, a Decree was made to new model the Regulations and Œconomy of *Jack's* Family in such Manner that they might for the Future be more subject to the Will of the Steward: And, thirdly, a large Gallows was erected before the Mansion House in the old Farm, and an Order made that if any of Jack's Children or Servants should be suspected of Misbehaviour, they should not be convicted or acquitted by the Consent of their Brethren, agreeable to the Purport of the *Great Paper,* but be tied Neck and Heels and dragged to the Gallows at the Mansion House, and there be hanged without Mercy.

No sooner did Tidings of this undue Severity reach the new Farm, but the People were almost ready to despair. They were altogether at a Loss how to act, or by what Means they should avert the Vengeance to which they were doomed: But the old Lady and Steward soon determined the Matter; for the *Padlock* was sent over, and without Ceremony fastened upon *Jack's* great Gate. They did not wait to know whether he would pay for the *Gruel* or not, or make the required Acknowledgments; nor give him the least Opportunity to make his Defence—The great Gate was locked, and the Key given to the old Nobleman, as had been determined.

Poor *Jack* found himself in a most deplorable Condition. The great Inlet to his Farm was entirely blocked up, so that he could [n]either carry out the Produce of his Land for Sale, nor receive from abroad the Necessaries for his Family.

But this was not all—His Father, along with the *Padlock*

---

by other measures (Intolerable Acts) giving extraordinary powers to the governor who could: transfer to British courts anyone indicted for a murder committed "in support of the laws of revenue"; appoint the provincial Council; choose sheriffs who in turn chose jurors; and decide whether a town meeting could be held. A Parliamentary measure of 1769 had already revived an obsolete statute under which a colonial governor could send to England any person charged with treason.

aforesaid, had sent an Overseer to hector and domineer over him and his Family;[20] and to endeavour to break his Spirit by exercising every possible Severity: For which Purpose he was attended by a great Number of Mercenaries, and armed with more than common Authorities.

On his first arrival in *Jack's* Family he was received with considerable Respect, because he was the Delegate of their aged Father: For, notwithstanding all that had past, the People of the new Settlements loved and revered the old Gentleman with a truly filial Attachment; attributing his [u]nkindness entirely to the Intrigues of their Enemy the Steward. But this fair Weather did not last long. The new Overseer took the first Opportunity of showing that he had no Intentions of living in Harmony and Friendship with the Family. Some of *Jack's* Domesticks had put on their Sunday Clothes, and attended the Overseer in the great Parlour, in Order to pay him their Compliments on his Arrival, and to request his Assistance in reconciling them to their Father: But he rudely stopped them short in the Midst of their Speech; called them a Parcel of disobedient Scoundrels, and bid them go about their Business.[21] So saying, he turned upon his Heel, and with great Contempt left the Room.

## CHAPTER VII

Now *Jack* and his Family finding themselves oppressed, insulted and tyrannised over in the most cruel and arbitrary Manner, advised with their Brethren what Measures should be adopted to relieve them from their intolerable Grievances. Their Brethren, one and all, united in sympathising with their Afflictions; they advised them to bear their Sufferings with Forti-

---

20. General Thomas Gage, commander of British forces in America, was named governor of Massachusetts in April 1774 and assumed office 17 May.

21. On 15 June, he interrupted the formal welcoming address of the Governor's Council, refusing to listen to "indecent reflections" on his predecessors, and two days later dissolved the House of Representatives. (*Pennsylvania Packet,* 14 July.)

tude for a Time, assuring them that they looked on the Punishments and Insults laid upon them with the same Indignation as if they had been inflicted on themselves, and that they would stand by and support them to the last. But, above all, earnestly recommended it to them to be firm and steady in the Cause of Liberty and Justice, and never acknowledge the *Omnipotence*

---

*Liberty Triumphant*

*A comical broadside of early 1774 celebrates the Boston Tea Party, reversing the map as if illustrating the popular song, "The World Turned Upside Down."*

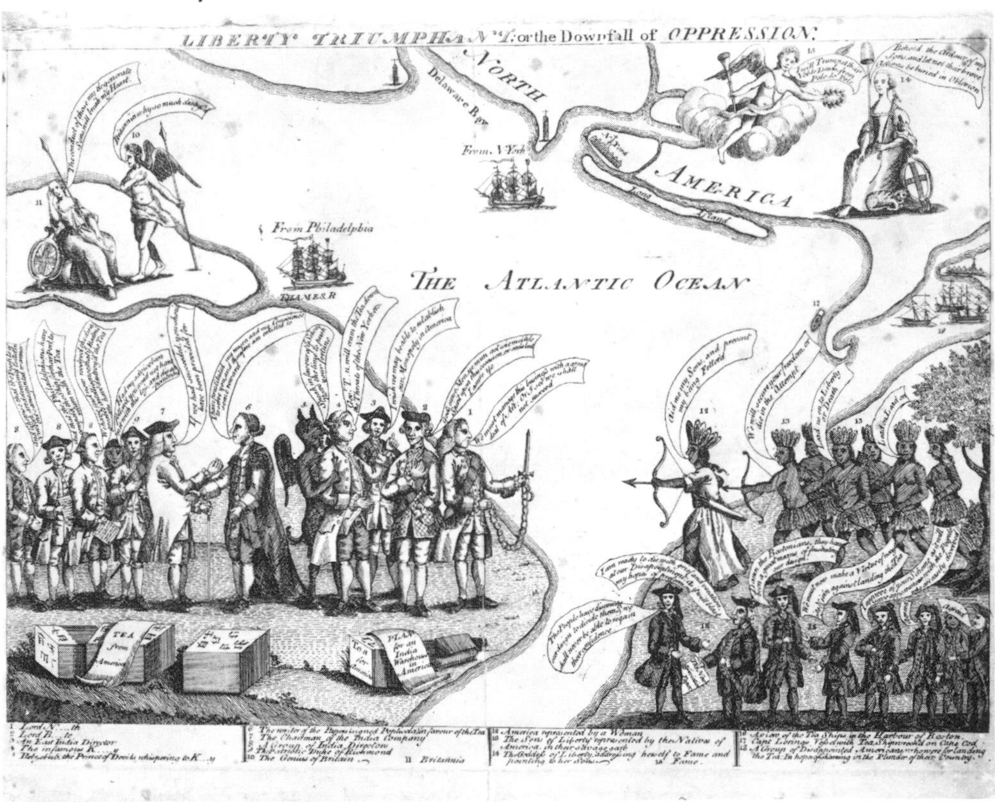

of their Mother in Law; nor yield to the Machinations of their Enemy the Steward.

In the mean Time, lest *Jack*'s Family should suffer for Want of Necessaries, their great Gate being fast locked, liberal and very generous Contributions were raised among the several Families of the new Settlements, for their present Relief. This seasonable Bounty was handed to *Jack* over the Garden Wall—All Access to the Front of his House being shut up.

Now the Overseer observed that the Children and Domesticks of *Jack*'s Family had frequent Meetings and Consultations together: Sometimes in the Garret, and sometimes in the Stable: Understanding, likewise, that an Agreement not to deal in their Father's Shop, until their Grievances should be redressed, was much talked of amongst them, he wrote a thundering Prohibition,[22] much like a Pope's Bull, which he caused to be pasted up in every Room in the House: In which he declared and protested that these Meetings were treasonable, traiterous and rebellious; contrary to the Dignity of their Father, and inconsistent with the *Omnipotence* of their Mother in Law: Denouncing also terrible Punishments against any two of the Family who should from thenceforth be seen whispering together, and strictly forbidding the Domesticks to hold any more Meetings in the Garret or Stable.

These harsh and unconstitutional Proceedings irritated *Jack* and the other Inhabitants of the new Farm to such a Degree that * * * * * * * * * * * * *

*Cætera desunt.*

22. The proclamation, 29 June, denounced Boston's "Solemn League and Covenant," a nonimportation agreement, as illegal—"scandalous, traiterous, and seditious"—and ordered the arrest of anyone circulating or signing it. (*Pennsylvania Packet*, 11 July).

# *FOR THE* PENNSYLVANIA MAGAZINE (1775-1776)

Encouraged by the popularity of *A Pretty Story*, and now having the leisure of a country gentleman, Hopkinson wrote satires regularly for the new *Pennsylvania Magazine* that began publication in Janary 1775. From the first number, Hopkinson was one of its steadiest contributors, submitting a stream of verse and light social satires after the fashion, still current, of Addison and Steele. Some of the poems were revisions of verse he had published as an undergraduate in his mentor William Smith's *American Magazine* a dozen years earlier. The essays, by contrast, seemed written for the occasion, but the contributions of a gentleman rather than a paid writer. They were anonymous even to the editor, who prefixed a note to the second of Hopkinson's pieces, "N. B. The future favours of this gentleman are requested." He complied with boundless abundance, providing verse and prose for almost every issue until the magazine ceased publishing with the number for July 1776.

Published by Robert Aitken, the *Pennsylvania Magazine; or American Monthly Museum* quickly achieved unprecedented circulation. About 1500 subscribed to its second number, all the more remarkable considering the unsettled state of public affairs. In the preface to the bound volume collecting the issues for 1775, Aitken lamented, "Those, whose leisure and abilities might lead them to a successful application to the Muses, now turn their attention to the rude preparation for war." But in his initial prospectus, he had promised to exclude controversy in politics or religion, as a means of attracting both subscribers and contributors without regard to faction. According to Hopkinson, signing himself "A. B." as he frequently would, this policy first attracted him: "You may perhaps wonder I have not tried my hand in some of the public papers; but the truth is, that what with your *Citizens*, your *Philadelphians*, your *Lovers of liberty*, and your *Lovers of no liberty at all*, your *Moderate men*, and *Immoderate men*, there is no such thing as getting a word or two in edge-wise . . ." (1:15).

From the beginning, Aitken featured engravings of men, music, maps, and machinery along with departments devoted to moral philosophy, history, book reviews, poetry, and "monthly intelligence" on current events in America and abroad. From the second number, his editor was Tom Paine, a recent immigrant whose only recommendation was a letter from Benjamin Franklin. In the early numbers, they repeatedly insisted on the promise of the prospectus to exclude political controversy, but, after the Battle of Bunker Hill in mid-June, the columns on "monthly intelligence" sparkled with patriotism for the colonial cause. The July issue contained a fervent essay on "defensive war" and Hopkinson's nonsatiric political essay, "On the Late Continental Fast." By the close of the first year, the original prohibition had been modified to apply only to local politics. The bound volume for 1775 featured an engraved title page showing the goddess of Liberty wearing a liberty cap, standing alongside a cannon resting on a huge ledger labeled "Congress."

The issues for 1776 left little doubt about the *Magazine's* radical politics, for besides articles on "Constitutional liberty" and maps showing the extent of British depredations in the south, there were detailed reviews of military textbooks providing copious extracts on military organization, tactics, and weapons for guerrilla warfare. The May number devoted a half-dozen columns to reviewing *A New System of Military Discipline*, giving exact instructions on how to defend a town under attack. The July number included the texts of the Declaration of Independence and also the new constitutions of New Jersey, Virginia, and Connecticut as models any other legislature could copy. That issue concluded with the promise that an engraving of New York harbor would appear "in our next." But, doubtless because of the shortage of paper—an increasing complaint in previous months—the July issue proved to be the last.

During its eighteen months' existence, Hopkinson published essays or poems in eleven issues. Of nine poems, four were riddles or answers, three were revisions of early verse. Of the previously unprinted poems none were political. Of his ten essays, only that on the Continental Fast was political. He did write and retain but not publish a bitterly invective "Prophecy," replying to a series of letters in the newspapers during April 1776 by William Smith writing under the name "Cato," urging a compromise with England at any cost. Hopkinson's parable accused him of being England's agent provocateur, practicing bribery and extortion. Whether these allegations were felt libelous or because events made reply superfluous, Hopkinson withheld the parable from the public.

Of the essays reprinted below, the initial "New Plan of Education," with its comical combination of fantasy and parody, uses a passage in a popular novel as a springboard for a graceful dive into fantastic pedagogy. The three sketches in the "Old Bachelor" series show Hopkinson at his best in dramatic satire, creating personae worthy to stand alongside Peter Grievous even though stripped of his political point. It was as though Hopkinson was leaving political satire to the professionals like Philip Freneau in verse and Tom Paine in prose, while he specialized in leavening the heavy times with light wit and sweet humor.

# *A NEW PLAN OF EDUCATION*

It hath long been a settled point, that few objects are of greater consequence to mankind than the proper culture of those who must in time supply the places of the present generation.

Very arduous is the task of Education both to the industrious teacher and his young disciples: Happy, therefore, is he who can contribute any thing towards rendering the road to knowledge easy and pleasant, or shorten the tedious length of the journey. Many schemes have been formed by ingenious men for this purpose; in which they have endeavoured to blend the *utile* and *dulce* in so intimate a connection, that the student may insensibly become learned, whilst he thinks he is only amusing himself. As I am quite willing to allow every person the merit due to his labours, I readily acknowledge the usefulness of their several devices: Such as teaching *Geography* by Maps cut into pieces, according to the divisions of countries, and pasted on wood; *Trade* and *Commerce* by a *Te-Totum; History* and *Chronology* by a Pack of Cards, and *Euclid's Elements* by solid figures in Box and many other similar inventions, by which science and mortality are planted in the youthful mind, by the fair hand of innocent pleasure.

The improvement I have made on this idea appears to me so important, that I am induced to offer it to the Public for the good of mankind; heartily recommending my plan to the serious consideration of the trustees of our college, and to the sanction of the legislature. I have herein not only united *Improvement* with *Delight,* but joined to them the invaluable blessing of *Health;* making these three desirable acquisitions to go hand in hand, improving and strengthening both body and mind by one amusing process.

This Preface, short as it is, hath, no doubt, already interested the curiosity of the reader. As I am not only willing to oblige every body when I can, but also to do it as speedily as possible; I shall not, like some authors, fill half a dozen pages in proving a self-evident proposition; or in setting forth, with laboured ingenuity, the advantages of a scheme, which, when known, must sufficiently recommend itself.

In order to execute my proposed plan, it will be necessary to purchase about twenty acres of land; which must be well cleared of all incumbrances. If this piece of ground be laid out in a circular form, it may be called *the whole Circle of Sciences;* wherein a great number of youths may be properly educated, and by a wholesome and profitable exercise, promote at once, health of body and instruction of mind.

To begin with *Grammar,* which costs the poor boys much trouble and attention: I beg leave to quote a passage from a late humorous Novel,[1] from whence, I must in justice acknowledge, I took the first hint of this improved plan of Education. The passage I allude to is this:

---

1. Richard Graves, *The Spiritual Quixote* (1773), 3:63–64. Graves was satirizing Locke's proposal "to teach Children to read, whilst they thought they were only Playing" (James Axtell, ed., *Educational Writings of John Locke* [Cambridge, 1968], p. 256).

Here, *Jockey*, let the gentleman *see* you decline the Pronoun Article *hic, haec, hoc.* Master *Jockey* immediately began hopping about the room, repeating *hic—haec—hoc;*—Gen. *hujus;* —Dat. *huic;*—Accus. *hunc—hanc—hoc;*—Voc. *caret;*—Abl. *hic—hâc—hoc.* There now, says *Selkirk*, in this manner I teach him the whole *Grammar.* I make eight boys represent the eight parts of Speech. The *noun Substantive* stands by himself; the *Adjective* has another boy to support him; the *Nominative Case* carries a little wand before the *Verb:* The *Accusative Case* walks after and supports his train. I let the four *Conjugations* make a party at whist; and the three *Concords* dance the *Hay* together and so on.

By this device, the common exercise of *Hop, Step,* and *Jump* is rendered truly Grammatical, and the head and heels are improved by one operation. In like manner, may the young scholar be instructed in *Arithmetic*, by the favourite play of *Hop-Scotch;* where certain squares are delineated with chalk on the ground, and inscribed with numerical figures. The dexterity lies in hopping about and kicking a piece of pot-sherd, or oyster-shell, with one foot, into the squares, so as to make the greatest amount of figures.

It is easy to conceive how, in such a commodious piece of ground, the several branches of the *Mathematics*, as *Trigonometry, Surveying, Navigation*, &c. may be acquired by actual exercise, in a mode very amusing to the students.

*Natural Philosophy* may be readily explained in the several sports in common use amongst boys. The *Vis Inertiae* and *Elasticity* of matter, and the general laws of *motion* will evidently appear in playing *marbles, fives* and *bandy-wicket:* The doctrine of *Projectiles*, the *accelerated* motion of descending bodies, and the *parabolic Curve;* the *centrifugal force* and the laws of Gravitation may be understood in shooting arrows, flinging stones and throwing snow-balls. *Pneumatics* will be taught in the use of the *Pop-gun; flying of kites; blowing bladders,* and lifting stones with a piece of wet leather and string: and *Hydrostatics* be explained by the *Squirt* and other aquatic amusements.

A compleat knowledge of *Logic* may be conveyed in the same entertaining manner. Let a large boy represent the *Major Proposition;* a small one the *Minor,* and a middle sized lad the *Conclusion.* Then let these three go play at *hide* and *seek* together: A *Sorites* may very aptly be represented by *thread my needle Nan;* and a *Dilemma* by *blind Buck and Davy.* Every species of *Syllogisms* may be instanced by devices of the like kind.

Thus far the sports in common vogue may be applied to the education of youth; but some ingenuity on the part of the tutor will be requisite to instruct them in *Moral Philosophy* and *Astronomy.* In order to the first, I would propose that the several *passions* and *affections* of the mind be represented by as many boys; each of which shall have his destined path and distance assigned by the tutor, who must himself represent *Reason.* These boys should all be blind-folded and started as for a race, and whilst they are running *helter-skelter* in full career, the tutor should exert himself with great vociferation in directing them to keep in their respective courses; calling out to one to stop, to another to push forward, and to all of them not to justle or interfere with one another. It will be requisite, that the strongest and most active boys should represent the *passions,* and the cooler *affections* of the mind be assigned to the young and tardy. Large stumbling blocks should be fixed at the ends of their respective courses, which will give them an idea of the office of *Conscience.* If an impetuous disciple should blunder over his stumblingblock, he ought to find himself entangled amongst briers and thorns, previously disposed for the purpose. The head scholar should be seated on high, as judge of the race, representing the *understanding,* and the strongest lad start the racers, emblematical of the *will.*

By this mode, after some additional improvements, may the whole of *moral Philosophy* be inculcated in athletic exercises, to the great delight of the youthful votaries of science.

To teach *Astronomy* it will be necessary to make use of the whole twenty acres of ground, which must be divided into concentric circles at proportionable distances for the courses of the heavenly bodies. Let the tutor fix himself as the *sun* in the centre; the larger boys represent the *Planets* and the smaller ones their *Satellites:* The teacher, with the help of a speaking trumpet, directing them how to perform their several periods in due order of time and place; which cannot fail of giving these *peripatetic* philosophers, an accurate idea of the solar system.

This is my proposed plan of education, and I doubt not but it will be approved by all ranks of people, and that it will not be long before I shall have the pleasure of seeing it carried into execution.

What an entertaining sight must it be to *see* the whole school performing their several *exercises.* Some *hopping* grammatically, *stepping* by mood and tense and *jumping* over pronouns and articles. If the young scholar should happen to lean too much on one side he may be said to be *declining;* and if he actually falls, will probably be in the *vocative;* by which it will appear he hath made some progress in his *Accidence* or rather *accidents.*—There is no person but must be highly delighted with such an exhibition.

In order to evince my own public spirit, I am determined, let the sum be what it will which our Assembly may be pleased to vote me as a reward for my ingenuity, I will apply every shilling of it to the purchase of the aforesaid twenty acres of ground.

*N.B.* It may be objected that the above plan is entirely calculated for fair weather only; but I am now preparing for the press the completion of my scheme by within door exercises: wherein I shall shew that *laws and government* may be taught by the play of *break the Friar's neck; Trade and Commerce* by *I am a Spanish Merchant;* the *Occult sciences* by *Hunt* the *Whistle* and *Hot Cockles* and so on.—But I will not, by anticipation, lessen the pleasure my readers will have in perusing my second-part of *Education improved.*

A. B.

*Volume I (March 1775), pages 101–04.*

# *CONSOLATION FOR THE OLD BACHELOR*

*By* Another Hand

Mr. Aitken,

Your Old Bachelor[1] having in a very picturesque and pathetic manner set forth the miseries of his solitary situation, severely reproaching himself for not having married in his younger days; I would fain alleviate his distress, by showing that it is possible in the nature of things, that he might have been as unhappy even in the desireable matrimonial state.

I am a tradesman in this city, and by unremitted industry am enabled, from the profits of my business, to maintain a wife and one daughter, now six years old, very comfortably, and to lay up a little at the year's end, against a rainy day.

My good wife had long teized me to take her to *New-York,* in order to visit *Mrs Snip,* the lady of a wealthy taylor in that city, and her cousin; from whom she had received many pressing invitations. This jaunt had been the daily subject of discussion at breakfast, dinner, and supper, for above a month before the time fixed upon for putting it into execution. As our daughter *Jenny,* could by no means be left at home, many and great were the preparations to equip Miss, and her mother too, for this important journey; and yet, as my wife assured me, there was nothing provided but what was absolutely necessary, and which we could not possibly do without—my purse sweat at every pore—At length the long expected day arrived, preceded by a very restless night; for as my wife could not sleep for thinking on the approaching jaunt, neither would she suffer me to repose

1. "The Old Bachelor" was a monthly feature from March through December, with about half the contributions unsigned. Although not numbered as part of the series, the "Consolation" elicited a reply in Number V, which in turn elicited Hopkinson's Number VI and Number VIII, the concluding essay in the series.

in quiet—If I happened through wearisomeness to fall into a slumber, she soon roused me again by some unreasonable question or remark; frequently asking me whether I was sure the apprentice had greased the chair-wheels, and seen that the harness was clean and in good order; often observing how surprized her cousin *Snip* would be to see us, and as often wondering how poor dear Miss *Jenny* would bear the fatigues of the journey. Thus passed away the night in *delightful* discourse—if that can properly be called a discourse wherein my wife said all that was said; my replies never amounting to more than monosyllables *Yes* or *No,* uttered between sleeping and waking.

No sooner was it fair day-light, but up started my notable wife, and soon roused the whole family. The little trunk was stuffed with baggage, even to bursting, and tied behind the chair, and the chair-box moreover crammed with trumpery—Miss *Jenny* was dressed, and breakfast eat in haste. The old negroe wench was called in, and the charge of the house delivered to her care—the two apprentices and the hired maid received many wholesome instructions and cautions for their conduct during our absense—all which they most liberally promised to observe. I waited with infinite patience the settlement of these preliminaries. At length, however, we set off, and turning the first corner, lost sight of our habitation, with great regret on my part, and no less joy on the part of my wife and Miss *Jenny.* When we got to *Poole's* bridge, there happened to be a great concourse of waggons, carts, &c. so that we could not pass for some time. Miss *Jenny* frightened—my wife very uneasy and impatient—wondered I did not call out to those impudent carters to make way for us, observing "that I had not the spirit of a louse—that I let every body impose upon me." Having at last got through this difficulty, we proceeded on our way without obstruction—My wife in good humour again—Miss *Jenny* in high spirits. At *Kensington* fresh troubles arose—Bless me, Miss *Jenny,* says my wife, where is the little band-box—"I don't know, mama—the last time I saw it, was on the table in your room."—What's to be done! the band-box is left behind—it contains Miss *Jenny's* new wire cap—there is no possibility of doing without it—as well no *New York,* as no wire cap—there is no alternative, we must e'en go back for it. Teized and mortified as I was, my good wife undertook to administer consolation, by observing, "That it was my place to see that every thing was put into the chair that ought to be—that there was no dependance upon me for any thing—that unless she looked after every thing herself, she was sure to find something neglected—and that she saw plainly, I undertook this journey with an ill-will, merely because she had set her heart upon it."—Silent patience was my only remedy—An hour and an half restored to us this valuable requisite, the wire cap, and brought us back to the place where the loss of it was first discovered.

After numberless difficulties and unparralelled dangers, occasioned by stumps, ruts, and tremendous bridges, we at length reached *Shammeny* ferry. But how to cross it was the difficulty—My wife protested that neither she nor *Jenny* should go over in the boat with the horse. I assured her in the strongest terms, that there was not the least danger—that the horse was as quiet as a dog. As well he might be, after tugging such a load. But the most forcible argument was, that she must go that way or not at all, as there was no other boat to be had. Thus persuaded, she ventured in.—The flies were troublesome; the horse kicked—my wife in panics—Miss *Jenny* in tears. *Ditto* at *Trenton* ferry. As we started very early, and the days were long, we reached *Trenton* by two o'clock. Here we dined—my wife found fault with every thing; ate a very hearty dinner—declaring all the time there was nothing fit to eat. Miss *Jenny* crying out with the tooth-ach, her mother making sad lamentations—all my fault, because I did not make the glazier replace a broken pane of glass in her chamber window—N. B. I had sent twice for him, and he promised to come; but he was not so good as his word.—After dinner proceeded on our journey. My wife in good humour. Miss *Jenny's* tooth-ach much better. Various chat—I acknowledge every thing my wife says for fear of discomposing her. We arrive in good time at *Princeton.* My wife and daughter admire the college—refresh ourselves with coffee—go to bed early, in order to be up by times for next day's expedition.

We embark once more in tolerable good humour, and proceeded happily on till we came to *Rocky Hill.* Here my wife's fears and terrors returned with great force. I drove as carefully as possible; but coming to a place where one of the wheels must unavoidably go over the end of a small rock, my wife in great panic seized hold of one of the reins, which happening to be the wrong one, she pulled the horse so as to force the wheel much higher up the rock than it would otherwise have gone, and overset the chair. We were all tumbled hickledy-pickledy into the dirt. Miss *Jenny's* face all bloody—the woods echo with her cries; my wife in a fainting fit, and I in great misery, secretly and devoutly wishing cousin *Snip* at the d____l.—Matters begin to mend. My wife recovers—Miss *Jenny* has only received a small scratch in her cheek.—The horse stands quite still, and none of the harness broke.—Matters grow worse again—The twine which tied the band-box had broke in the fall; and the aforesaid wire cap was found soaking in a nasty mud-puddle. Great lamentations over the wire cap—all my fault, because I did not tye it better. No remedy—no wire caps to be bought at *Rocky Hill.* At night my wife discovered a small bruise upon her hip—was apprehensive it might mortify—did not know but the bone was broke or splintered—many instances of mortifications arising from small injuries. After passing unhurt through the imminent dangers of *Passayeek* and *Hackensuck* rivers, and the yet more dreadful horrors of *Powlas Hook* ferry, we arrived on the third day at cousin *Snip's* in the city of *New-York.*

Here we tarried a tedious week. My wife spent me a great deal of money in purchasing a hundred useless articles, which *we could not possibly do without;* and every night when we went to bed, fatigued me with encomiums on her cousin *Snip,* leading to a history of the grandeur of her family, and concluding with reproaches thrown at me for not treating her with as much homage and respect as I ought. On the seventh day, however, my wife and her cousin *Snip* had a very warm debate, respecting the comparative elegancies and advantages of the cities of *New York* and *Philadelphia.* The dispute ran very high, and many aggravating words passed between the two advocates. The next morning my wife declared that my business absolutely required my attendance at home, and that it was not possible for us to stay any longer. After much ceremonious complaisance, in which my wife was by no means exceeded, we left the famous city of *New York,* and I with great satisfaction look forward to the wishful period of our safe arrival in *Water-Street.* But this blessing was not so easily to be purchased. Lest I should seem tedious, however, I shall not recount the adventures of our return; how we were caught in a thunder gust; how our horse tired, by which we were benighted above three miles from our stage; how my wife's panics returned; how Miss *Jenny* howled; and how very miserable I became. Sufficient be it to say; that after many distressing disasters, after much vexation and trouble, we at length arrived at our own door.

No sooner had we entered the house, but we were informed that one of the apprentices had gone off with the hired maid, no body knew where,—the old negroe wench had got drunk, fallen into the fire, and burned out one of her eyes,—and my wife's best china bowl was broke to pieces. My wife's usual ingenuity contrived to throw the blame of all these misfortunes upon me. As this was a consolation to which I had been long accustomed in all untoward cases, I had recourse to my usual remedy, to wit, silent patience.—And after sincerely praying that I might never see cousin *Snip* again, I sat down industriously to my trade; endeavouring to retrieve my manifold losses.

This is only a miniature picture in the decorations of the married state, which I hold up to the view of your Old Bachelor, in hopes it may tend to abate his choler, and reconcile him in some degree to a single life.

If this opiate should not be sufficient to give him some ease and comfort, I may perhaps hereafter administer a stronger dose:

or rather, to resume my former metaphor, shall send him a picture of the married state more at length, and taken from the life.

In the mean, I am
His and your humble servant,
A. B.

*Volume I (June 1775), pages 254–57.*

# *THE OLD BACHELOR*

*Number* VI

Oh! that I had been made an oyster! that I had been stationed in the bottom of the sea! The winds might have blown their utmost; they might have swelled the waves mountains high, I should have heeded them not. Mankind might have been satiated with folly, deceit, and iniquity, it would not have troubled me: But what is more than all the rest, I should have propagated my species in a numerous offspring, without the help, without the plagues, without the expence of a female assistant.—

Here some journey-man-philosopher would interrupt me with a learned dissertation on sexes, and, by a chain of irrefragable *suppositions*, prove that oysters are male and female.—What's that to you, Sir? Who asked your opinion on this matter? The deuce is in these cox-combs that they cannot let a man go on his own way, but they must be throwing straws across his path. Go, Mr. Philosopher, about your business.—Go, catch butterflies, and search for the pineal gland of a musketoe.

Oh that I had been made an oyster! 'Tis true I should forfeit what are called the enjoyments of life; that is, I should not eat turtle soup and venison, 'till I nauseated both, nor drink Madeira and claret 'till my head aked—true—neither should I be tormented with the treachery of servants, the hypocrisy of relations and nominal friends, or the insults and sarcasms of my fellow oysters.

You should have heard from me before this, Mr Aitken, but I

have been sick—very sick—almost at the point of death. I caught cold by putting on a damp shirt. If I had been married, my wife, perhaps, would have taken care that my linen should be well aired—perhaps not—be this as it may, I was very sick; no body troubled their heads about me; I lay helpless, languishing and neglected above, my servants rioted and plundered below: Every thing went into confusion. The common comforts of the sick were not administered to me. I lay many hours alone, given up to my own melancholy reflections. I thought I should die: I supposed myself dead—I saw my own funeral—Not a single tear to embalm my memory. A few straggling neighbours attend the scanty procession, conversing on politics as they follow me to the grave. —The following day some person in the next street asks one of my near neighbours, "How does the old bachelor? I hear he is sick?"—"He was sick, but he is well enough now; he was buried yesterday."—"Dear me! I never heard it; how has the old Curmudgeon left his estate?"—"To the Pennsylvania hospital." —No more is said about me—they pass on to other chat. After three days I am no more remembered than if I had never existed —except by the managers of the Pennsylvania hospital.—No widow to be visited and comforted for the loss of me; No children to keep my name and memory alive in the world, and to talk of their father some ten or a dozen years after my decease: No elegies, either in verse or prose, to celebrate the virtues I never possessed, or apologize for the faults I really had; not even a paragraph in a news-paper to announce my departure—Yes, I had some comfort in supposing that my name might creep into the fag end of your magazine, under the List of Deaths, with a declaration that I had left my estate to the Pennsylvania hospital.

Such was the dismal train of ideas that presented to my imagination. My disorder increased. My life was despaired of. Some half a dozen second and third cousins came to see me. They disgusted me with their officious, overacted kindnesses. "Why did not you send, my dear cousin, to let me know you was sick?" cries one.—"I never heard a word of it till this morning; I came the moment I was informed of your danger," says another;—"Do take this,—pray try that—there is nothing better for a fever; I have known it do wonders; Mr. Such-a-one was given over by the doctors, and recovered by the use of it."—Another of my very loving relations sat down by my bedside, and with a dismal face, began to expatiate on the uncertainty of life; and then, after a few common place observations, and half a dozen hem's and haw's and inward groans, he came to the main point he had in view,—"I hope, my dear cousin, said he, that you have settled your worldly affairs; your loving relations expect it of you—I hope you have made your will—these things had better not be delayed—It will be an ease to your mind when that necessary business is done, and you will not die a bit the sooner for having compleated it. We all hope you may recover, God grant you may! but, as we are all mortal, and know not how soon we may be called upon, it is prudent to provide against the worst."—I told him that my will was already made, and that I had no inclination to alter it.—They continued to teize me with unremitting cruelty. My strength was so exhausted that I could not scold, and storm, and swear, as I wished to do.—I fretted inwardly—My physician too was in league with my cousins; he denied me every thing I desired, and forced upon me every thing I loathed and abhored. My situation was truly deplorable—I earnestly wished for a draught of cool water—I requested it in terms of the most pathetic solicitation; but in vain. At length, however, I prevailed on an old negro wench, who is not worth a farthing, and yet the most valuable servant I have, to convey privately to me a tankard of water, fresh from the pump. I drank it off greedily. It threw me into a profuse sweat, and a deep sleep.—It saved my life.—I began to recover from that time. No sooner was I out of danger, but my loving cousins, who had not been to see me for four years preceding my illness, left me with one consent; and it is very probable, they will not come to see me again for four years to come. Heaven grant they may not!—But I fancy I need not be under any apprehensions on that score, as they will discover by this paper, that I have left my estate to the Pennsylvania hospital.

Such is the forlorn state of an old bachelor; sick or well there is none that will do him a service, or even a common act of civility, but from the most interested motives. I sometimes wish I had married when I was young, but when I look round amongst my acquaintance, and see an insulting tyrannical wife, a reprobate spend-thrift son, and a daughter running off with the first vagabond that offers, I hug myself in my solitary state, and bless my stars, that I did not marry when I was young.

Upon the whole, I *find* so many reasons to wish I was a married man, and *see* so many reasons to rejoice I am not, that I am like the pendulum of a clock, hanging in suspence, and perpetually vibrating between two opinions. Notwithstanding all the fine things that have been said, time out of mind, about the married state, I am persuaded that he who marries must venture boldly. It is not a subject that will bear much reasoning upon. Ninety nine times out of a hundred it is passion not reason that points to matrimony. Should a man before he engages, call up to his view all the disasters, troubles, and inconveniences, which probably may, which certainly must, occur in the married state, he would never have courage to undertake the task. In my youthful days, I fancied myself in love two or three times. I even made considerable advances towards a courtship; but I reasoned too much on the consequences, and therefore remain, as you see, a fretful *Old Bachelor*.

C.

*Volume I (October 1775), pages 455–57.*

## THE BACHELOR

### Number VIII

I might have sat in my elbow-chair 'till doomsday, and revolved the matter over, and over, and over again, 'till my brain had become as dry as a box of Scots snuff. I might have wasted the midnight lamp, read all the works of the ancients and moderns, the learned and the unlearned on the subject, and even out-studied *Duns Scotus* himself, yet I should not have been able to determine the point.—'Tis very strange, said I, that any speculation whatever should be supported and counter-acted, established and confuted, by reasons so exactly ballancing each other, as to leave the judgment hanging in air, like Mahomet's coffin—The hundred thousandth part of a grain would set all a-going; and yet, I cannot throw that hundred thousandth part of a grain into one scale, but I find as much hath dropped into the opposite; and I am left just where I was.—In short, I found it impossible to determine *whether I had better marry or not.*

At last, *an accident*—who could have thought it!—*an accident* settled this important matter—broke the dam which I had been many years building up, strengthening, and repairing, and let out all my objections at once in a torrent. It would have surprised any one to see how my *prudential motives*, *self-love*, *avarice*, *pride*, *pecularities of opinion*, &c. &c. &c. tumbled out *helter-skelter, head over heels*, like the breaking up of a play-house. Here, you might have seen *pride* flouncing and bouncing indignant through the foaming tide;—there, lay *avarice* wrigling and twisting in mud and slime:—In one place, *self-love*, like a mud-turtle collected within its own dirty shell, and thousands of *odd notions* and *peculiarities of opinion* crawling about every where like snails, wood-lice, tod-poles, and a variety of unformed vermin.

But the *accident* which occasioned this extraordinary revolution, is worth recounting,—you shall hear it—

In my last I informed you of my illness, and recovery: For the better establishment of my health, the exercise of walking was much recommended. Accordingly, I made it a rule, whenever the weather would permit, to walk two or three miles before dinner. One day, in taking my usual exercise, I crossed the Commons, and found myself in the lower ferry road. Two women passed me in a chair. The youngest of the two drew the attention of a momentary glance. I thought I discovered something in her, that made me wish for a longer view. They had not proceeded above an hundred yards when their horse took fright, ran up against the fence, and over-set the chair. I made all the haste I could to the assistance of the unfortunate ladies. The elder of the two seemed to have received no great injury from the accident; but the younger, either from the force of the fall, or through fear had fainted away. I took her in my arms. Her head reclined on my bosom. She was delicate—she was beautiful. I felt an anxiety I never felt before. Love, though I knew it not, stole into my heart, in the disguise of compassion. I chafed her temples, her wrists, and the palms of her hands. The soft touch thrilled through every vein, and awakened unusual sensibilities. —She recovered, and, observing her situation, with a gentle effort disengaged herself from my arms; then thanked me for my care with graceful ease, and a languishing voice. The elder lady, who I found was her mother, joined her in grateful acknowledgments. The horse and broken chair were left at a neighbouring house, and I insisted on conducting the ladies home. Little passed during this walk but grateful expressions on the part of the ladies, and polite assurances on mine. I did not fail, however, to examine the young lady's person and deportment with eager attention, and the more I examined the more I was pleased with her. As they were both much discomposed by the accident, I did not choose to intrude upon them at that time; but took my leave at their door with a promise to wait on them next day and enquire after their health.

After I returned home, this adventure engrossed all my thoughts. I secretly wished myself some twenty years younger, that I might with propriety endeavour to make this amiable young lady all my own.—What a treasure, said I to myself, must she be to a man of sense and delicacy! How happy should I be at this time, if I had, in the earlier part of life, connected myself with such an engaging companion! But I have missed the golden opportunity, and must e'en *fret* out the remainder of my life as well as I can.—

The day was long—the night longer. The next morning was chiefly spent in preparations for my afternoon's visit. I was uncommonly particular about my dress, although I had no determined design in view. The barber had express orders respecting the dressing of my wig; my best suit of broad-cloth was taken out of the press; and my new beaver neatly and carefully brushed;—in short, I was more attentive to my dress for this visit, than I had been for many years before: But I satisfied myself by placing all to the score of politeness and civility.—When all was ready I went to the glass to adjust my wig. I thought I looked uncommonly well; at least I observed a neatness in my dress, and a vivacity in my countenance, to which I had been long unaccustomed. Certain reflections arose in my mind, which I could not *then* suppress. And thus I reasoned with myself—Few men carry their age better than I do—this must be owing to the regularity and temperance of my past life—a discreet man of *fifty* hath the powers of life in greater vigour than a debauché of *twenty*.—Who knows what may happen?—perhaps—Oh the enchanting idea!—stranger things have come to pass—My fortune is unexceptionable, my person, I think not disagreeable, and my constitution rather better since my late illness than before. At this instant I took up my hat, which lay on the table close by an old quarto family Bible: The corner of my hat in lifting, took the upper cover of the Bible, and threw it back; when, behold, on the first leaf of the aforesaid Bible, these words, in legible characters, saluted my eye—*George, the son of Thomas and Alice Sanby* was born in the *city of London*, on the 10th of October *anno domini* ****—I need not give you the figures; suffice it to say that this malicious accident had a great effect upon my mind: It lowered the top-sails of my vanity in a moment, and dispersed all the gay ideas I had assembled before me. I left home somewhat disconcerted. Many jarring sensibilities distracted my mind, 'till I got to the house where I was to make my visit.

It is time to inform you that the mother of this young lady keeps a small shop in ——— street, upon the profits of which, and the interest of a thousand pounds left her by her deceased husband, she maintains herself and her only daughter. Her husband had been a merchant of some note; but, partly by losses in trade, and chiefly by living too expensively for his income, he had it not in his power to leave his family any thing considerable at his death. This intelligence I artfully got from a friend in the common way of chat.

I was received by my new friends with the utmost cordiality and respect. The mother was all complaisance and civility; the daughter all sweetness and innocence, heightened by a pleasing vivacity. Our discourse first turned upon the accident of the preceding day. I was happy in finding it attended with no bad consequences to the ladies; and happier still (as I took care to observe) that it was the means of introducing me to such agreeable acquaintance; declaring, at the same time, my intention of taking all the advantage it afforded, by paying my respects to them in occasional visits. To this a reply was made quite to my satisfaction. In short, I spent the afternoon and a good part of the evening most agreeably.—I returned home in high spirits, much enamoured with the young lady's person, deportment and amiable disposition as far as I could discover it on so short an acquaintance. I thought no more on the accident of the family Bible; but indulged myself the remainder of the evening in a thousand golden dreams.

I amused myself next day with writing this letter; but, if ever you expect to hear from me again, I must insist upon it, that you do not intitle this, or any subsequent letter, The *old* Bachelor; but only *The Bachelor*. I am not so old perhaps, as you may imagine. I dare say Methuselah at my age was only in leading strings, and beginning to cut his teeth. A man as hearty and ruddy as I am, cannot with any propriety, be called *old*. *Old* philosopher, *old* hermit, *old* conjurer, *old* married man, may be expressions proper enough; but, I insist upon it, the epithet *old* should never be applied to a bachelor, unless he is a great deal older than I am yet—thank God!—You may alledge that in some of my letters I have called myself the *Old Batchelor*—true—but I was then not well and a little low-spirited. I have a right to recall the expression. Indulge me in this particular, and you may hear from me again.

C.

*Volume I (December 1775), pages 551–54.*

# FOR THE PATRIOTIC PRESS (1776-1780)

During the late spring of 1776, Hopkinson was deep in a struggle that wrested control of the New Jersey legislature from the Loyalists. Elected to Congress in late June, he dashed to Philadelphia to cast the colony's vote for the Declaration of Independence, then worked so devotedly on congressional committees that he rejected appointment as associate justice of New Jersey's supreme court. In November he assumed the first in a series of administrative and judicial posts (often served concurrently): Chairman of the Navy Board, Treasurer of Loans, Judge of the Admiralty Court of Pennsylvania and, when that post was abolished in 1789, Judge of the United States Court for the Eastern District of Pennsylvania. During these hectic times, he still maintained active interest in music, science, and drawing—designing, for instance, the Stars and Stripes. He also somehow managed to publish satires almost every year.

During 1776–81, while serving on the wartime Navy Board and as the harassed Treasurer of Loans trying to cope with runaway devaluation of Continental currency, he published at least ten effective satires in verse and prose. In prose, he mocked the portentous threats of British generals, ruminated on the ruinous policies of the British empire, and focused public attention on the potentially ruinous threat from homegrown Tories. In verse, his "Battle of the Kegs" celebrated a hilarious incident he himself had incited to embarrass British forces occupying Philadelphia (from September 1777 to July 1778)—most timely propaganda inasmuch as Americans had grown fearful of

British superiority in arms, and Hopkinson turned that fear to laughter at the enemy's own psychoses.

In other verse, he focused on the Tory threat, a clear and present danger to the infant nation, militarily, fiscally, and ideologically. After the British evacuated Philadelphia, many Loyalists remained as spies or suspected spies, providing information or supplies, often speculating in currency and otherwise subverting the economy. Even conscientious

---

*"Mal Lui Veut Mal Lui Tourne" (?1780)*

*Illustrating a pseudo-Poor Richard proverb, that wishing ill to others brings it on oneself, this tableau reflects France's hope that the war would ruin English trade. While other nations milk American profits (3) from the British cow (1) and Congress dehorns her (2), the British fleet blockades Philadelphia (6 & 7), an Englishman wrings his hands in futile distress (9), and the British lion naps (8).*

Quakers who refused to take an oath of allegiance to America on religious grounds were suspect. A Tory presence in Philadelphia, seat of the national government, was cause enough for alarm. But an added anxiety was the attitude of Philadelphians generally. After the British left the city, the war raged on fiercely elsewhere, yet Philadelphians returned to normalcy, as though their war were over.

At the close of 1779, General Washington, visiting the city, was outraged at the citizens' conduct. He saw them given over to "speculation, peculation, and an insatiable thirst for riches."[1] When they should have been patriotic, they were parochial: "Party disputes and personal quarrels are the great business of the day whilst the momentous concerns of an empire, a great and accumulated debt; ruined finances, depreciated money, and want of credit . . . are but secondary considerations and postponed from day to day, from week to week as if our affairs wore the most promising aspect."

It was against this attitude that Hopkinson directed his satires as the decade concluded, wishing that he could do more or that others would help. Reporting to Benjamin Franklin on the effectiveness of their political squibs, he lamented that other satirists would not join them: "Ammunition of this kind hath been rather scarce with us. Most of our Writers have left the great Field of general Politics, wherein they might have been of considerable Service to skirmish & bush-fight in the Fens & Thickets of Party Dispute."[2] But he was confident that his own work had been effective in attacking the enemy, and now wished it would be just as effective in redirecting American minds to the national interest.

During these anxious years, his favorite vehicle was the *Pennsylvania Packet,* published in Philadelphia by John Dunlap, who had printed the *Pretty Story* and also the Declaration of Independence. Dunlap's was the only Philadelphia paper to publish consistently during the war. On 4 July 1776, the city boasted six—the *Packet, Gazette, Journal, Evening Post,* and *Staatsbote* were patriotic; the *Ledger,* Tory. With the occupation, the *Evening Post* also turned Tory and, except for the *Packet,* the other patriotic papers ceased publishing. Dunlap followed Congress into exile, printing his paper in Lancaster. Though Congress revived the *Gazette* at York as official organ, the *Packet* too printed official documents alongside its wonted miscellany of news, information, and patriotic propaganda from all over America and abroad.

1. George Washington, *Writings of Washington,* ed. J. C. Fitzpatrick (Washington, 1936), 13:467.
2. George Hastings, *Life & Works of Francis Hopkinson* (Chicago, 1926), p. 279.

As the leading light of the patriotic press in Pennsylvania, the *Packet* provided other American papers a fruitful source of official news and unofficial propaganda such as Hopkinson's. Thus, whether he wrote directly for the *Packet* or for other papers such as Burlington's *New Jersey Gazette*, Hopkinson could be confident of wide dissemination in the patriotic press.

# *I AM A TORY*

Mr. Towne,

I am a Tory, the son of a Tory, born and bred in the principles of absolute submission, and a true friend to the Hanoverian family; whom I will ever support, right or wrong, through thick and thin. The King of Great Britain hath, in my humble opinion, authority, *jure divino,* to govern *absolutely* not only that small island with its appendages, but the East and West Indies; not only the East and West Indies, but the continent of North-America; not only the continent of North-America, but the whole of this insignificant planet—*if he can.* For pray, Mr. Towne, what could this poor world, called the earth, have been made for, unless it be to aggrandize the aforesaid Hanoverian family. The infatuated people of this vile part of this most vile planet (the whole of which is indeed unworthy the acceptance of his *most gracious Majesty*) have been moved by the instigations of the Devil to resist and oppose his royal desire of governing them *in all cases whatever.* For my part, I am struck with horror at the very thought of this rebellious opposition. *His most gracious Majesty* hath, however, to my great consolation, sent over certain fleets and armies to reduce this abominable country to his subjection. Now it becomes the friends of arbitrary government to afford all the assistance to the said fleets and armies they possibly can, and to the worthy Lords and Generals whom the said gracious King hath appointed to direct and manage the same. Amongst other implements of war, the *pen* and the *printing-press* are not the least important. It is true they break no bones and shed no blood, but they can instigate others to do both; and, by influencing the minds of the multitude, can perhaps do more towards gaining a point than the best rifle gun or the sharpest bayonet.

On these considerations I have been long anxious to see a printing-press in this city subservient to the purposes of *Lord and General Howe*—I am gratified—I am happy in finding the said great men have, at length, found out a printer to their mind, and much good may be expected from it. I was mentioning this to a friend, whom I thought a Tory like myself—but I was mistaken in my man. He had the assurance, Mr. Towne, to address me in the following manner on the subject—I will give it you as near as I can in his own words; that you may see what sort of men we have amongst us.

"Sir," says he, "it has been the policy of every government, from the beginning of time, to this day, when the honor, safety and existence of that government depended on the fate of war, to use every possible means to strengthen and support its own efforts, and counteract the subtleties and force of those who seek its destruction. For this purpose many of the most sacred rights of the people have been hard prest and even boldly violated, and that without any danger to the constitution itself; provided the exertions of government be manifestly sanctified by the necessities of the case. To prove this, we need only advert to the constant practice of the British court, in pressing men for supplying the navy in times of war. A measure rather winked at than authorised by the constitution, and a high infringement on the liberty of the subject. But the emergencies of war have been ever deemed a sufficient justification of this and many other deviations from the line of the constitution.

"The liberty of the press hath been justly held up as an important privilege of the people. It is indeed highly reasonable that the channels of information should be kept open for the benefit of the multitude; and no man holds this right in more sacred estimation than I do. But when this privilege is manifestly abused, and the press becomes an engine for sowing the most dangerous dissentions, for spreading false alarms, and undermining the very foundations of government, ought not that government, upon the plain principles of self-preservation, to silence, by its own authority, such a daring violator of its peace, and tear from its bosom the serpent that would sting it to death.

"What I have now in view is the *Ledger* of last Saturday, in which is pompously displayed large extracts from the *New-York Mercury;* a paper published under the immediate influence of our inveterate enemies; in which facts are misrepresented, reason distorted, the power and feats of the enemy exaggerated, and all the force of falsehood exerted, to do that by subtlety which they are not able to effect by strength. The design of the printer in publishing these extracts must be too evident to admit of a doubt. The printer of the *Pennsylvania Ledger* must be either a friend to the cause of America, or a cool, indifferent, impartial man, or a well-wisher to the enemies of his country, commonly called a *Tory.* In one or other of these characters he must appear, and I think it is impossible to hesitate long in assigning him his proper department, when we consider the general complexion of the *Pennsylvania Ledger.* Why then should a fatal lenity protect a man in the abuse of that very lenity which is his only security? And would not the Council of Safety of this state be very justifiable in silencing a press whose weekly labors manifestly tend to dishearten our troops, to throw disgust on the friends of America, and hold up in false and glaring colours the characters and performances of those whose only errand is the total destruction of this country? But if that Honorable Council should be loth to exert an authority of which they may have some doubts, the public ought at least to shew their resentment against such an insidious enemy, by refusing to take a newspaper fraught with mischief, and continually aiming at the demolition of their peace; I believe there is no government would suffer so dangerous a publication to be continued one week, but ours; and I am satisfied *Lord Howe* does not permit extracts from our papers to appear in the *New-York Mercury,* unless they are taken from the *Pennsylvania Ledger,* or are such as may favor the object he has in view."

This, Mr. Towne, was the purport of his speech. I was shocked at his assurance, and determined to have no more connexion with him.

A TORY.

*The Pennsylvania Evening Post, 16 November 1776.*

## *SOCIETY OF TORIES*

Mr. Towne,

It is not easy to conceive how much I was surprised and disappointed at the discourse of my friend, as communicated to you in my last. There is indeed no knowing whom to trust in these times, and people should be very cautious how they open their minds to men of a doubtful political character. It is a maxim in our society of *Tories* to be very circumspect in this particular; but I confess I was taken in, in this instance, and have had the mortification of being reprimanded for my indiscretion at a full meeting of our society: But as my friend in Front-street was in the chair, I came off as well as I could expect.

You can't imagine what regularity and method prevails in our body; we are all formed into Committees of various denominations, and appointed for various uses. I have the honor to belong to the Committee of Wiles and Stratagems. It was I, Mr. Towne, who lately planned and executed the scheme for stealing from an express certain letters and despatches from General Washington to Congress; and you may depend upon it that whilst the Committee of Congress were searching Bristol for those letters, they were on their way to our friend *General Howe;* where they arrived safe, as we have been since informed. You may be sure I gained great applause for this manœuvre.

We have two other Committees, the one called a Committee of *False Reports,* whose business it is to fabricate and publish such articles of supposed intelligence as may best serve the purpose of alarming the timid, and distracting the minds of the people. These are given out at such times as the various circumstances of public affairs may render them most probable, and are some times circulated, by whispers, in so secret a manner, that their origin cannot be traced; and at other times, openly, by means of the *Pennsylvania Ledger:* The other is called the Committee of *True Intelligence,* whose business it is to employ proper persons as spies: These are directed to mix amongst the people in the characters of *Whigs,* and to hire themselves as servants and waiters in such houses and taverns as are frequented by Members of Congress. They also employ emissaries to keep up a communication with Lord and General Howe, which is done under various masques and disguises.

Happily for us, the several stages and ferries have been quite free; so that our messengers have passed and repassed unexamined, and this department hath as yet been attended with little or no difficulty. We have also a Committee of *Lies;* whose duty differs from that of *False Reports* in this; the one misrepresents facts respecting the movements of the armies, and things of a public nature, the other only devise temporary *lies,* respecting what passes in this city, and particularly as to the deliberations and intentions of Congress. These lies must be fresh and fresh every other day, and are always backed with a strong assertion that the *information came from a Member of Congress.*

Another Committee is the Committee of *Extortion,* it is their part to monopolize as far as they can the articles necessary for the rebel army, and to hold up at high prices all the necessaries of life, in order to make the people discontented and uneasy.

The last Committee I shall mention, is the *Depreciating Committee*—as useful a Committee, Mr. Towne, as any. It is their business to devise ways and means to depreciate the Continental currency, and persuade the people that it is of no value, but will sink in their hands, to their utter ruin. This Committee is very large, and composed chiefly of monied men.

Their artifice is to collect Continental currency, and immediately discharge with it such bonds and debts as they may have contracted, with a seeming anxiety to get it out of their hands as fast as they can. If they have goods to sell, they affix three prices to them; one if the buyer will pay in hard money, a higher price if paid in Provincial currency, and a still higher if paid in

Continental bills of credit. But they have many other ways of bringing that currency into disrepute, which I am not at liberty to mention. I would also give you a list of the men of most influence and ingenuity amongst us, and I assure you the catalogue would be very respectable, but I am not permitted to do it now, whatever I may do hereafter, when Toryism may be more safely and openly avowed.

We hold frequent meetings at different places; some times at our friends in Front-street, some times at particular taverns in the city, and some times in the suburbs. Be assured we spare no pains to bring our affairs to a happy issue; and though some folks may think, nay, do not scruple to declare that we are doing all we can to ruin the country, and entail a miserable slavery on our posterity, yet we are satisfied we are doing the best we can for ourselves, and hope to enjoy the *heart-felt* satisfaction of seeing our former neighbours and friends imprisoned or hanged by hundreds, or their estates confiscated, and the owner turned out to beggary and want, whilst we enjoy our lives and possessions, and, perhaps, are promoted to high honors. If this should not be the case, there is no gratitude in government, and no faith in Lord Howe. I am yours, &c.

A TORY.

*Pennsylvania Evening Post, 26 November 1776.*

# *LETTER BY A FOREIGNER*

Translation of a Letter written by a Foreigner, on his Travels.

London, Dec. 3, 1776

Dear Count,

I have now been six months in England, and eight weeks of the time in or near this metropolis. You should have heard from me before, but my frequent excursions and continual avocations, as well as the want of a proper opportunity, prevented. Agreeable to my promise, however, I now sit down to give you some account of the character and politics of this strange people. So copious a subject cannot be discussed in one letter, but you shall hear from me again when further observation hath enabled me to be more particular.

The general character of the English is certainly the most absurd and fantastic that ever fell to the lot of human nature. As they are made up of contradictions it would be unjust to describe them by any uniform designation. There is scarce a virtue that adorns the mind, or a vice that disgraces mankind but may be ascribed to them as a nation: But the former are often rendered ineffectual by misapplication, and the latter qualified by a levity of manners that shews them not to be constitutional. An Englishman will treat his enemy with great generosity and his friend with ingratitude and inhumanity. He will be lavish of his wealth, when he has but little; and become a miserly wretch, when Fortune pours her riches into his purse. He will brave the utmost hardships and suffer the severest trials of life with heroic patience; and will drown himself because the wind is in the East. He will lend large sums to a stranger on the slightest security; and will go to law with his nearest relation to wrong him out of his estate. To-day his heart expands with social benevolence; to-morrow he is cold, sullen and reserved. To-day he possesses the wealth of a Nabob; to-morrow he refuses a groat to a beggar.—In short, contradiction and absurdity make an Englishman.

During the last century, this people have risen to a great height of wealth and power; but the instability of their temper will not suffer them to enjoy any blessing in possession. At peace with all the world; feared and respected by their neighbours; daily enjoying the benefits of an extensive and uninterrupted commerce; an established policy and a reformed religion, are circumstances sufficient, one would suppose, to render any people happy and content. But the thirst of lawless ambition can never be satisfied. —The English assume to themselves the character of being the most *just, generous* and *humane* nation in the world: And yet they carry on the *African trade;* a trade attended with circumstances of cruelty and horror that are a disgrace to human nature;

whereby they fasten, for life, the chains of misery and servitude on some hundreds of their fellow creatures every year. They also sent one Clive over to the East-Indies to establish a dominion there. A country which the Creator never designed should belong to the English, as is evident from his having placed it on the opposite side of the globe, and made the inhabitants of a different complexion. This Clive, however, arrived with his forces in the East Indies; and, under sanction of his *most gracious* Majesty and a *free* Parliament, put to death some hundred thousands of the inhabitants by the sword, by famine and by the most attrocious cruelties—and so returned to England with immense riches and a wife set in diamonds, and was made a Lord; and then with great deliberation he cut his throat with a pen knife, to the satisfaction of the whole Court.—You will be surprised at this: But the people here are not surprised at all. It is no unusual thing to spend an evening with a great man in all the easy gaity of social-life, and to hear next morning that he had hanged himself in a stable, or practised phlebotomy with a razor on his own jugular vein. The English now govern in the East-Indies with a supremacy of power, and a tyranny so pure and unalloyed with any mixture of justice or humanity, as could not have been exceeded in the reigns of the *twelve Caesars.*

This exploit being accomplished to the glory of God and honour of the nation; this *just, generous* and *humane* King turned his attention to AMERICA. There he had three millions of subjects who lov'd, honour'd and obey'd him. He govern'd them by men of his own nomination; he had the whole regulation of their commerce, and the overflowings of their wealth were conducted by easy and natural channels to his coffers and to the purses of the merchants and manufacturers of his kingdom. But he has quarelled with this people, because they are so stupid that they cannot understand, or so obstinate that they will not acknowledge that *two and two make five.* Volumes have been written on this subject, and all the force of reason and eloquence exerted to convince this wise King that he is in an error. The Americans have most emphatically beseeched him to accept of the undisguised loyalty of their hearts, declaring that they are satisfied that the fruits of their industry should, *as heretofore,* center with him and his people to enrich and aggrandize them; but humbly request that they may not be compelled to acknowledge that *two and two make five,* which would be a most distressing violation of truth; as they know and are fully convinced that they make only *four.*

But this *humane* Monarch is far from giving up the point. He has rejected their petitions with scorn, and spurned at their offers of affection and fidelity. He declares he will even risque the crown of his ancestors but he will make the obstinate Americans own this new doctrine.

To be as good as his word, he hath sent over not only his own fleets and armies, but hired a banditti of foreign mercenaries from a petty Prince, who maintains himself and family by the merchandize of human blood, and has also employed Negroes and wild Indians to persecute the poor Americans without mercy until they shall own that *two and two make five.*

America is now a scene of desolation and distress. A theatre whereon is acted a real tragedy enriched with every species of cruelty and injustice. The royal army are ravishing the women, murdering the men, and laying waste that beautiful country under the conduct of *Lord and General Howe,* who are cajoling some and ruining others of these inoffensive people, with all the composure in the world. His most gracious Majesty receives from time to time such accounts of their proceedings as they please to give him, and is as happy as such a Monarch can be. Who could have thought that so extensive a country would be ravaged and plundered because the foolish inhabitants will not own that *two and two make five,* when their good King and his wise Parliament desire them to do so? Especially when the consequence of so doing can be only the utter ruin of themselves and their posterity forever.

But this is not all. The Americans, highly resenting this treatment, have declared before God and the world that they will be no longer pensioners of the smiles or frowns of such a King, or dependant on the justice or humanity of a Sovereign who pays no regard to either; but that they are determined to be henceforth a free people, and will enjoy the inestimable privilege of believing and saying that *two and two* make only *four,* agreeable to the common sense of mankind. How this affair will terminate is a matter of some uncertainty. But the chance is *ten* to *one* that George the Third will lose the most glorious jewel of his crown, if not the crown itself, for this ridiculous whim, this *ignis fatuus* in politics.

You will say, the King could not act upon such absurd principles, were he not countenanced and supported in his folly by the co-incident folly of his people.—True—but the folly of the people is of a different nature from that of the King. The people see plainly with the Americans, that *two and two* can never make *five,* and yet they support his Majesty's *dogma* with might and main. The truth is, they have by degrees resigned so much power into the King's hands that they dare not now contradict any thing he shall please to assert. And if his power should be further encreased by the subjection of America to his disposal, the ruined people of England may bid adieu to their constitution for ever. Some of the wisest amongst them see this, and have declared that the salvation of England depends on the success of the Americans in the present war. This infatuated people have tired the world for these hundred years with loud eulogiums on liberty and their constitution, and yet they daily see that very constitution languishing in a deep consumption without any efforts for it's recovery. Instead of enjoying a frame of government beautiful in her proportions and glowing with health and vigour, they are content to embrace a rotten prostitute full of wounds and bruises and putrifying sores. Amused with trifles, and long accustomed to venality and corruption, they are not alarmed at the dreadful consequences. They love to talk of their beloved constitution because the idea is agreeable; and they honour their King because it is the fashion. They worship the shadow of Liberty with an idolatrous adoration, neglecting the substance as a thing of no value. Half the loyalty of the nation is supported by two popular songs, viz. *God save the King,* and *Britons strike Home.* These are vociferated at taverns, over porter, punch and wine, till the imagination is heated and the blood in a ferment, and then the worthy patriots stagger forth and commit all manner of riots and excess in honour of their King and country. There are fanatics in politics as well as religion, and persecution is the consequence in both, when men refuse to attend to the cool dictates of common sense. The men in power know this weakness of the multitude; and whenever they find them grow uneasy under their encroachments, they get half a dozen court scribblers to expatiate on the blessings of the British constitution, and sing the sweet lullaby of Liberty to the people to keep them quiet. Just as a nurse rattles three pieces of tin in a little rush basket to amuse her crying child: The poor infant thinks it has the world in possession, and is satisfied.

The English are not a people of an inventive genius. Most of their able men are natives of other countries. The Scotch far exceed them in literature; and, in the arts, France and other nations invent for them, and they improve upon their inventions. Few useful arts owe their origin to native English. The Quadrant, called *Hadley's Quadrant,* was undoubtedly the contrivance of an *American,* tho' *Hadley* assumed the reputation of that discovery. They were in high luck when a *Shakespear* and a *Newton* happened to be born amongst them. The whole nation rest their credit upon these two men.

The extreme ignorance of the common people of this *civilized and polished* country is scarcely to be credited. They know nothing but the particular branch of business to which their parents or the parish happened to put them apprentice. They are compelled to practice *that* with unremitting diligence, and beyond *that* they seldom extend their ideas. A manufacturer has been brought up a maker of pin-heads. He has been at it forty years, and of course he makes them with great dexterity; but he cannot make a whole pin for his life. He thinks it is the perfection of human nature to make pin-heads. He leaves other matters to inferior abilities. It is enough for him that he believes in the Athanasian Creed, reverences the splendor of the Court, and makes pin-heads. This he esteems the sum total of religion, politics and trade. He is sure that London is the finest city in the world; Black-Friars the most magnificent of all possible bridges, and the river Thames the largest river in the universe.—It is in vain to tell him that there are many rivers in America in comparison of which the Thames is but a ditch; that there are single provinces there larger than all England, and that the colonies formerly belonging to Great-Britain, now Independent States, are vastly more extensive than England, Wales, Scotland and Ireland taken together. He cannot conceive this. He goes into his best parlour and looks at a map of England five feet square; on the other side of the room he sees a map of North and South-America not four feet square, and cries, *How can this be? It is altogether impossible!*—He has read the Arabian Nights Entertainment, and he hears this wonderful account of America. He believes the one as much as the other. That a giant should rise out of the sea, or that the Delaware should be a larger river than the Thames, are equally inconceivable to him. Talk to him of the British Constitution, he will tell you it is a glorious one; he adores it. Ask him what it is, and he does not know even its first principles. Mention the freedom of elections, and he will tell you he has no business with these matters—that he lives in a borough, and that it is impossible but that *'Squire Goosecap* must represent that borough in Parliament; for his lady comes every Sunday to the parish church in a damask gown, and sits in a pew lined with green cloth—how then can it be otherwise?—Besides, *'Squire Goosecap* is acquainted with the Prime Minister. These are things he is in no ways concerned in. He believes in the Athanasian Creed, is astonished at the splendor of the Court, and makes pin-heads —and what more can be expected of man?—

It is quite otherwise in America. The lowest of the people there are not without some degree of general knowledge. They turn their hands to every thing. Their situation obliges them to do so. A farmer cannot run to an artist upon every trifling occasion. He must make and mend and contrive for himself. This I observed in my travels thro' that country.—In many towns and in every city they have public libraries. Not a shoe-maker or a taylor but will find time to read. He acquires knowledge imperceptibly, and gets a love for books—He reads voyages and travels, and becomes acquainted with the geography, customs and characters of other countries. He studies the first principles of government, he knows the great outlines of his rights as a free man, as a citizen, and is proud of the character; not as an empty name, but for its substantial benefits. He amuses himself a little with astronomy, and knows that the apparent motion of the Sun is occasioned by the real motion of the Earth. In short, he knows that, notwithstanding the determination of King, Lords and Commons to the contrary, *two and two can never make five.*

Such are the people of England and such the people of America. They are now at daggers drawn. At first the Americans knew little or nothing of warfare; but they improve daily. The British troops are teaching them the art of conquest, and they find them very apt scholars. The probable consequence is that England will lose and America gain an empire. If *George* III. should subjugate America on his present principles, all good men will abhor him as a tyrant; if he should not, all the world will laugh at and despise him for throwing away the immense advantages he enjoyed in a friendly connection with that country, because the inhabitants will not acknowledge that *two and two make five,* agreeable to his royal will and pleasure.

But it is time to conclude this long letter, lest I should tire your patience and my own. For the present, therefore, adieu, and believe me to be as much as ever

Yours, &c. &c. &c.

*Pennsylvania Packet, 4 February 1777.*

# *TO JOHN BURGOYNE*

*To* John Burgoyne, *Esquire, Lieutenant-General of his Majesty's armies in America, Colonel of the Queen's regiment of light dragoons, Governor of Fort William in North-Britain, one of the Representatives of the Commons of Great Britain, and command-*

*ing an army and fleet employed on an expedition from Canada, &c &c*[1]

*Most high, most mighty, most puissant and sublime General!*

When the forces under your command arrived at Quebec in order *to act in concert and upon a common principle with the numerous fleets and armies which already display in every quarter of America the justice and mercy of your King,* we the reptiles of America were struck with unusual trepidation and astonishment. But what words can express the plenitude of our horror when the *Colonel of the Queen's regiment of light dragoons* advanced towards Ticonderoga. The mountains shook before thee, and the trees of the forest bowed their lofty heads—the vast lakes of the North were chilled at thy presence, and the mighty cataracts stopped their tremendous carreer and were suspended in awe at thy approach.—Judge, then, *oh ineffable Governor of Fort William in North Britain,* what must have been the terror, dismay and despair that overspread this paltry Continent of *America* and us it's wretched inhabitants. Dark and dreary, indeed, was the prospect before us, till, like the sun in the horizon, your most gracious, sublime and irresistible proclamation opened the doors of mercy, and snatch'd us, as it were, from the jaws of annihilation.

We foolishly thought, blind as we were, that your gracious master's fleets and armies were come to destroy us and our liberties; but we are happy in hearing from you—and who can doubt what you assert? that they were *called forth for the sole purpose of restoring the rights of the constitution to a forward and stubborn generation.*

And is it for this, Oh sublime *Lieutenant-General,* that you have given yourself the trouble to cross the wide Atlantic, and with incredible fatigue traverse uncultivated wilds?[2] And we un-

1. The issue of the *Packet* in which this essay appeared carried Burgoyne's proclamation itself, dated 2 July 1777, four days before he captured Ticonderoga. The italicized phrases are direct quotations from the proclamation.
2. In fact, Burgoyne was moving down from Canada to join General Sir William Howe's forces at Philadelphia in a movement that could have defeated the

gratefully refuse the profer'd blessing?—To restore the rights of the constitution you have called together an amiable host of Savages and turned them loose to scalp our women and children, and lay our country waste—this they have performed with their usual skill and clemency, and we yet remain insensible of the benefit and unthankful for so much goodness.

Our Congress have declared independence, and our Assemblies, as your Highness justly observes, have most *wickedly* imprisoned the avowed friends of that power with which they are at war, and most *profanely* compelled those, whose consciences will not permit them to fight, to pay some small part towards the expences their country is at in supporting what is called a necessary defensive war. If we go on thus in our obstinacy and ingratitude, what can we expect but that you should, in your anger, *give a stretch to the Indian forces under your direction—amounting to thousands, to overtake and destroy us;* or, which is ten times worse, that you should withdraw your fleets and armies and leave us to our own misery, without compleating the benevolent task you have begun, in *restoring to us the rights of the constitution.*

We submit—we submit, most puissant *Colonel of the Queen's regiment of light dragoons, and Governor of Fort William in North Britain!* We offer our heads to the scalping-knife and our bellies to the bayonet. Who can resist the force of your eloquence? Who can withstand the terror of your arms? The invitation you have [given in the consciousness of Christianity, your royal master's clemency, and the honour of soldiership] we thankfully accept. The blood of the slain, the cries of injured virgins and innocent children, and the never ceasing sighs and groans of starving wretches, now languishing in the gaols and prison-ships of New-York, call on us in vain whilst your sublime proclamation is sounded in our ears. Forgive us, oh our country! Forgive us dear

---

Americans once and for all. But in October, harassed and slowed by American troops, Burgoyne would run out of supplies and, surrounded, surrender—an event that would boost American confidence and convince France that the revolution could succeed and was thus worth supporting. General Howe, meanwhile, would occupy Philadelphia from September 1777 into June 1778.

posterity! Forgive us, all ye foreign powers who are anxiously watching our conduct in this important struggle, if we yield implicitly to the persuasive tongue of the most elegant *Colonel of her Majesty's regiment of light dragoons.*

Forbear then, thou magnanimous *Lieutenant General!* Forbear to denounce vengeance against us—Forbear to *give a stretch* to those *restorers of constitutional rights, the Indian forces under your direction.*—Let not *the messengers of justice and wrath await us in the field, and devastation, famine and every concomitant horror* bar our return to the allegiance of a Prince who, by his royal will, would deprive us of every blessing of life, with all possible clemency.

We are *domestic,* we are *industrious,* we are *infirm and timid:* we *shall remain quietly at Home and not remove our cattle, our corn or forage,* in hope that you will come at the *head of troops in the full powers of health, discipline and valour* and take charge of them for yourselves. Behold our wives and daughters, our flocks and herds, our goods and chattels. Are they not at the mercy of our Lord the King and of his *Lieutenant General, Member of the House of Commons, and Governor of Fort William in North-Britain?*

Saratoga, 10 July, 1777

A. B.
C. D.
E. F. &c &c &c

*Pennsylvania Packet, 26 August 1777.*

# *THE BATTLE OF THE KEGS*

Official records show that Hopkinson himself initiated the event he celebrated in his most famous ballad. He was serving as Chairman of the Navy Board when, exiled to Burlington from British-occupied Philadelphia, he ordered his father-in-law's cooperage to construct a number of kegs filled with powder and designed to explode on contact as they floated down the river. These ingenious mines were launched a few miles above Philadelphia early in January 1778. But the British ships had been docked to protect them from the ice, and the kegs passed harmlessly by—except for one that was pursued by curious lads. The fate of those lads was reported in the *Pennsylvania Ledger,* a loyalist paper, on 11 February 1778, in a monitory preface to a hilarious report (doubtless by Hopkinson) reprinted from the *New Jersey Gazette:*

> The town not being so fully acquainted with the subject of the following letter, taken from the Burlington paper, as the ingenious author would have his readers believe them to be, it may be necessary to relate them the fact;—at the time it happened it was so trifling as not to be thought worthy of notice in this paper,—and we do not doubt but our readers will allow this letter-writer full credit for the fertility of his invention:— The case was, that on the 5th ult., a barrel of an odd appearance came floating down the Delaware, opposite the town, and attracted the attention of some boys, who went in pursuit of it, and had scarcely got possession of it, when it blew up, and either killed or injured one or more of them very much. So far the matter was serious, and the fellow who invented the mischief may quit his conscience of the murder, or injury done the lads, as well as he can. Some days after, a few others of much the same appearance, and some in the form of buoys, came floating in like manner, and a few guns were, we believe, fired at them from some of the transports lying along the wharfs;—other than this, no notice was taken of them, except indeed by our author, whose imagination, perhaps, as fertile as his invention, realized to himself, in the phrenzy of his enthusiasm, the matters he has set forth.
>
> BURLINGTON, *Jan.* 21.
>
> *Extract of a Letter from Philadelphia, Jan.* 9, 1777. [sic]
>
> "The city has lately been entertained with a most astonishing instance of the activity, bravery, and military skill of the royal navy of Great Britain. The affair is somewhat particular, and deserves your notice. Some time last week two boys observed a keg of a singular construction, floating in the river opposite to the city, they got into a small boat, and attempting to take up the keg, it burst with a great explosion, and blew up the unfortunate boys. On Monday last several kegs of a like construction made their appearance—An alarm was immediately spread through the city—Various reports prevailed; filling the city and the royal troops with consternation. Some reported that these kegs were filled with armed rebels; who were to issue forth in the dead of night, as the Grecians did of old from their wooden horse at the siege of Troy, and take the city by

surprize; asserting that they had seen the points of their bayonets through the bung-holes of the kegs. Others said they were charged with the most inveterate combustibles, to be kindled by secret machinery, and setting the whole Delaware in flames, were to consume all the shipping in the harbour; whilst others asserted that they were constructed by art magic, would of themselves ascend the wharfs in the night time, and roll all flaming thro' the streets of the city, destroying every thing in their way.— Be this as it may— Certain it is that the shipping in the harbour, and all the wharfs in the city were fully manned—The battle began, and it was surprizing to behold the incessant blaze that was kept up against the enemy, the kegs. Both officers and men exhibited the most unparralled skill and bravery on the occasion; whilst the citizens stood gazing as solemn witnesses of their prowess. From the Roebuck and other ships of war, whole broadsides were poured into the Delaware. In short, not a wandering chip, stick, or drift log, but felt the vigour of the British arms. The action began about sun-rise, and would have been compleated with great success by noon, had not an old market woman, coming down the river with provisions, unfortunately let a small keg of butter fall over-board, which (as it was then ebb) floated down to the scene of action. At sight of this unexpected reinforcement of the enemy, the battle was renewed with fresh fury—the firing was incessant till the evening closed the affair. The kegs were either totally demolished or obliged to fly, as none of them have shewn their *heads* since. It is said that his Excellency Lord Howe has dispatched a swift sailing packet with an account of this victory to the court at London. In a word, Monday the 5th of January 1778, must ever be distinguished in history for the memorable BATTLE OF THE KEGS.

Hopkinson's ballad appeared in the *Pennsylvania Packet* 4 March, then being printed in exile at Lancaster, without preface or preliminaries of any kind.

BRITISH VALOUR DISPLAYED
Or, The BATTLE of the KEGS

Gallants attend, and hear a friend
  Trill forth harmonious ditty;
Strange things I'll tell, which late befel
  In Philadelphia city.

'Twas early day, as Poets say,
  Just when the sun was rising;
A soldier stood on a log of wood
  And saw a sight surprising.

As in a maze he stood to gaze,
  The truth can't be deny'd, Sir;
He spy'd a score of kegs, or more,
  Come floating down the tide, Sir.

A sailor too, in jerkin blue,
  This strange appearance viewing,
First damn'd his eyes in great surprize,
  Then said—"some mischief's brewing:

"These kegs now hold the rebels bold
  "Pack'd up like pickl'd herring,
"And they're come down t'attack the town
  "In this new way of ferrying."

The soldier flew, the sailor too,
  And scar'd almost to death, Sir,
Wore out their shoes to spread the news,
  And ran 'til out of breath, Sir.

Now up and down throughout the town
  Most frantic scenes were acted;
And some ran here and others there,
  Like men almost distracted.

Some fire cry'd, which some deny'd,
  But said the earth had quaked;
And girls and boys, with hideous noise,
  Ran thro' the streets half naked.

*Sir William* he, snug as a flea,[1]
  Lay all this time a snoring;
Nor dreamt of harm, as he lay warm
  In bed with Mrs. *Loring.*[2]

Now in a fright he starts upright,
  Awak'd by such a clatter;
First rubs his eyes, then boldly cries,
  "For God's sake, what's the matter?"

At his bed side he then espy'd
  *Sir Erskine* at command, Sir;[3]
Upon one foot he had one boot
  And t'other in his hand, Sir.

"Arise, arise," *Sir Erskine* cries,
  "The rebels—more's the pity!
"Without a boat, are all afloat
  "And rang'd before the city.

"The motley crew, in vessels new,
  "With Satan for their guide, Sir,
"Pack'd up in bags, and wooden kegs,
  "Come driving down the tide, Sir.

"Therefore prepare for bloody war,
  "These kegs must all be routed,
"Or surely we despis'd shall be,
  "And British valour doubted."

---

1. Sir William Howe led the British troops that occupied Philadelphia on 27 September 1777.
2. Whatever its basis in fact, this allusion strikes at Joshua Loring, a loyalist refugee from Boston, appointed by General Howe early in 1777 to be commissary of prisoners, and accused of excessive cruelty.
3. Sir William Erskine, one of Sir William's generals.

The royal band now ready stand,
All rang'd in dread array, Sir,
On every slip, in every ship,
For to begin the fray, Sir.

The cannons roar from shore to shore,
The small arms make a rattle;
Since wars began I'm sure no man
E'er saw so strange a battle.

The *rebel* dales—the *rebel* vales,[4]
With *rebel* trees surrounded;
The distant woods, the hills and floods,
With *rebel* echoes sounded.

The fish below swam to and fro,
Attack'd from ev'ry quarter;
Why sure, thought they, the De'il's to pay
'Mong folks above the water.

The kegs, 'tis said, tho' strongly made
Of *rebel* staves and hoops, Sir,
Could not oppose their pow'rful foes,
The conqu'ring British troops, Sir.

From morn to night these men of might
Display'd amazing courage;
And when the sun was fairly down,
Retir'd to sup their porridge.

One hundred men, with each a pen
Or more, upon my word, Sir,
It is most true, would be too few
Their valour to record, Sir.

---

4. The *Royal Pennsylvania Gazette,* the Tory newspaper, habitually referred to "rebel army" and "rebel transactions."

Such feats did they perform that day
Against these wicked kegs, Sir,
That years to come, *if they get home,*
They'll make their boasts and brag, Sir.

*Pennsylvania Packet, 4 March 1778.*

## *DATE OBOLUM BELISARIO*

The title of this poem is an obvious allusion to a saying "Date obolum Belisario" attributed to the great general Belisarius who, in his old age, was neglected by Emperor Justinian but permitted to beg in the streets—a saying that appeared in colonial newspapers with increasing frequency, applied to fallen greatness.

As late I travell'd o'er the plain,
About the close of day
I chanc'd to wander in a lane,
A lane of mire and clay.

'Twas there a dirty drab I saw,
All seated on the ground,
With oaken staff and hat of straw,
And Tatters hanging round.

At my approach she heav'd a sigh,
And due obeysance paid;
Fi[r]st wip'd a tear from either eye,
Then her petition made.

"A wretch forlorn, kind Sir, you see,
"That begs from door to door—
"Oh, stop and give, for charity,
"*A Penny to the Poor!*"

"Tho' now in tatters I appear,
"Yet know the time has been
"When I partook the world's good chear,
"And better days have seen."

Proceed, said I, whilst I attend
The story of thy woe—
Proceed, and charity shall lend
Some help before I go.—

"If blooming honours men delight,
"If charms in wealth they see;
"My Fame once soar'd a glorious height;
"And who more rich than me?

"Of sons and daughters I can boast
"A long illustrious line;
"Of servants could command a host,
"For large domains were mine.

"But George, my youngest, faithless boy,
"Hath all my powers o'er thrown,
"And in the very beds of joy
"The seeds of sorrow sown.

"He, thirsting for supreme command,
"Contemn'd my wise decrees;
"And with a sacrilegious hand
"My dearest rights did seize.

"A magic wand I once possess'd,
"A cap aloft it bore,
"Of all my treasures this the best,
"And none I valued more.

"Ruthless, he broke the sacred rod,
"The cap he tumbled down;

"Destroying thus what, with their blood,
"His ancestors had won.

"An Orphan child fell to my care,
"Fair as the morn was she,
"To large possessions she was heir,
"And friendly still to me.

"But *George*, my son, beheld the maid
"With fierce, lascivious eye:
"To ravish her a plan he laid,
"And she was forc'd to fly.

"She's gone—and will no more depend
"On cruel *George* or me:
"No longer now my boasted friend,
"Nor of my family.

"Bad measures often end in worse—
"His fell intent to gain,
"He sent, in rage, a mighty force
"To bring her back again.

"But to protect the injur'd Maid
"Her faithful Household came;
"In battle strong they stood array'd,
"And gain'd immortal fame.

" 'Mongst these a god like Hero rose,[1]
"Wise, generous and brave;
"He check'd the fury of her foes,
"His arm was strong to save.

"So near perfection, that he stood
"Upon the bound'ry line

1. George Washington.

"Of finite from infinite good,
"Of human from divine.

"Defeated thus, in all his schemes,
"My foolish, wicked son
"Awak'd from his delusive dreams,
"And found himself—*undone*.

"Mean while, I suffered in disgrace;
"No comfort could I find:
"I saw distress come on apace,
"With ruin close behind.

"At length, distracted quite with grief
"I left my native home;
"Depending now on chance-relief,
"Abroad for bread I roam.

"A shield and lance once grac'd these hands—
"Perhaps you've heard my fame,
"For I was known in distant lands—
"BRITANNIA is my name.

"BRITANNIA now in rags you see,
"I beg from door to door;
"Oh, give, kind Sir, for charity,
"*A Penny to the Poor!*"

*Pennsylvania Packet 22 April 1778.*

# *AN ADDRESS TO THE INHABITANTS OF CONNECTICUT*

On 20 July 1779, the *Pennsylvania Packet* printed without comment a proclamation made on the Fourth of July by Admiral Sir George Collier and General William Tryon offering amnesty to citizens of Connecticut who would cease and desist "the ungenerous and wanton

Insurrection" disturbing the peace of the continent: "Your towns, your property, yourselves, lie still within the grasp of that power, whose forbearance you have ungenerously construed into fear. . . ." The *Packet* for 22 July pointed out that this proclamation was held in universal ridicule for threatening citizens at a time when the tide of war now flowed against the British. But the writer did not mention that Admiral Collier and General Tryon had proceeded to raid the Connecticut coast, burning Fairfield and Norwalk and setting fire to shipping in New Haven harbor. Hopkinson's unsigned poem in the same issue, however, satirizes both British insolence and "mercy" as it versifies statements from the 250-word proclamation. The version in the posthumous *Miscellaneous Essays* omits about a third of the original.

Well may you fear, oh wretched crew!
The vengeance dire to traitors due:
For lo, we come with lash in hand,
To scourge and purge this guilty land.
Yet stay—let's have some conversation
E'er we proceed to flagellation;
As pedagogues sometimes make speeches
Whilst they let down their pupils breeches.
BURGOYNE did so at Saratogue,
Addresses now are all in vogue,
And General HOWE in Jersey too,
Spread proclamations not a few:
For, tho' the condescension's great,
We do vouchsafe sometimes to treat,
And take great pains with long haranguing,
To save our caitiff necks from hanging:
But you, to your own int'rests blind,
Remain ungrateful and unkind.
And tho' we warn you o'er and o'er,
Are still as stupid as before;
Are like the adder deaf, precisely,
Altho' the charmer charms so wisely.
'Tis true, and take it on our word,
If you'll submit to George the Third,

You'll surely find it better far,
Than carrying on this bloody war.
The consequence is only this,
And sure it is not much amiss,
You'll be of slaves a happy nation,
From generation to generation.
And what is that, compar'd with all
The mischiefs which may now befall,
If you, rebellious, still persist in
This naughty practice of resisting.

Yourselves, your towns, you can't deny,
Within the grasp of power lie;
And that we can, with greatest ease,
Clap paw upon you when we please.
That you've a house to put your head in,
Have pots or kettles, beds or bedding,
Is to our great forbearance owing,
And tender mercies ever flowing.
What you, presumptuous, call your own,
You only have from us on loan:
When we demand it back again,
You know resistance must be vain.
Therefore your houses, goods and land,
As monuments of mercy stand.[1]

But we have hopes you now begin
To see your fault and own your sin.
The very *Continent*, we're told,
Begins to blush[2]—tho' late so bold:
Is conscious of its many crimes,
And therefore would repent by times.

---

1. The proclamation read: "You, who lie so much in our power, afford the most striking Monument of our Mercy . . . ."
2. "The greater part of this Continent begins to blush . . . ."

And surely 'tis a thing uncommon
For fields to blush like any woman;
For rocks and trees to turn quite red,
Like girl for loss of maidenhead;
Or mountains, rivers, plains and vallies,
To look like thieves condemn'd to gallies.

But you who thus at mercy lie,
Should first to our protection fly,
And save yourselves from fell perdition,
The sad reward of black sedition.
Would you do this, 'twould be a sample
For others—and the good example
Might draw in many worthy folks
To poke their necks into our yokes,
And so become—Oh blessed thing!
The servants of our gracious King.

And here, we think it not amiss
To leave you to reflect on this;[3]
And do most manfully declare,
That we will all those culprits spare
Who stay at home in peace and quiet,
Disclaiming this unnat'ral riot:
We'll spare their dwellings—and what more is,
Be kind as HOWE to Jersey tories.
But rebels of the military
Must still remain in sad quandary,
And those who fill departments civil
Will sure go headlong to the devil;

3. "Leaving you to consult with each other upon this invitation; We do now declare,—that whosoever shall be found, and remain in peace, at his usual place of residence, shall be shielded, either to his person, or his property; excepting such as bear offices either civil or military, under your present usurped Government."

Unless they will their follies own,
And pardon ask on marrow-bone.

Think not, because we now are kind,
We shall be always of one mind;
And that our goodness has no end,
Because as yet we've been your friend.
Should you perversely still proceed
We shall be very wrath indeed:
And when we're angry—you know what—
*Connecticut* must go to pot:
Too late you'll find yourselves mistaken,
And not a man will save his bacon.
Our rage will then like light'ning fall,
And—lord ha' mercy on you all.
We'll neither spare old age or youth,
But firk and jerk you to the truth.
Therefore beware!—you may rely on
The words of COLLIER and of TRYON.
P. S. As 'twill be dark thro'out the land,
Before this letter gets to hand;
For your convenience we propose,
And out of love sincere—God knows,
To fire some houses—three or four—
And they perhaps may kindle more:
That by so great a blaze of light
You may see our intentions right,
And clearly read, tho' it be night.

A.B.

*Pennsylvania Packet 22 July 1779.*

## HIGH COURT OF HONOUR

Behind this modest proposal lay a four-year controversy on the conduct of medical affairs in the American army. Dr. John Morgan, a brother-in-law of Hopkinson, was appointed Director-General and

Chief Physician in 1775 but was dismissed for inept administration in January 1777. To vindicate his administration, he published a 158-page pamphlet exposing a cabal of medical officers who had undermined him in the eyes of Congress. That cabal was led by Dr. William Shippen, Jr., appointed by Congress to succeed him. In June 1779, Morgan finally obtained a formal court-martial of Shippen on charges of misconduct, especially for speculating in hospital supplies and medicine. But in August, Congress dismissed the charges, reappointing Shippen to his post. Morgan then appealed to public opinion through the columns of the *Pennsylvania Packet*, opening them to a flood of charges and countercharges in almost every issue from 2 September through 23 December when Hopkinson's essay closed the controversy, in the *Packet* at least. Other papers printed renewed charges and countercharges from time to time until Shippen resigned in 1781 and, nominated for the post, Morgan turned it down.

Having observed, with real concern, that our News papers have for a long time past, been filled with private contest and calumny, to the great abuse of the liberty of the press and dishonour of the city: I, who have been ever ambitious of devising some thing for the public good, never before devised or thought upon by any schemer whatever, set my wits to work to remedy this growing evil, and restore our Gazettes, Advertisers, Packets, &c. to their original design, viz. to make them vehicles of intelligence, and not the common sewers of scandal. To convince you that I am not altogether unqualified for this great design, I would inform you that I have had a tolerable education in the charity school of the University. My parents, being poor, bound me out to a scrivener; my master soon discovered in me an aptitude for business, and as I wrote a good hand, took me from the menial labours of the kitchen and cellar into his office, where I engrossed deeds, leases, wills, &c. and, in a word, did the chief business of his office. After I was free I became a clerk to several successive mayors, aldermen and justices of the peace; and to my honour be it spoken, my employers frequently applied to my judgment in difficult points, and, with due deference, I may say, that my advice contributed, not a little, to support their worships official reputation. But to proceed to my project, which, after much labour and study, I have compleated, and now offer to the public, without any prospect of reward; further than the reputation of being the author of so ingenious and salutary a scheme.

Let there be a new court of justice established, by the name and stile of the HIGH COURT OF HONOUR, to consist of twelve impartial and judicious persons, to be elected annually by the freemen of the state; in which election all persons, of whatever degree or quality soever, shall be entitled to a vote, strangers only excepted, who have not resided one year in the city or county where they would vote. The court, when met, to appoint a suitable person to be their clerk. This court shall have jurisdiction in all matters of controversy, between man and man, of what kind soever they be, provided no property, real or personal, comes in question: They shall determine on differences in opinion, points of honor, ceremony, rank and precedence; in all cases of affronts, slights, abuse, scandal, slander, calumny, and in all matters of contest, except as before excepted: Nine judges shall make a quorum, and a majority of voices shall determine the judgment of the court; and from their decision there shall be no appeal: The clerk shall keep a large book, to be called the RASCAL'S RECORD; in which shall be fairly entered, alphabetically, the name, occupation, and place of residence of any person on whom the judgment of the court shall fall; which book shall at all times be open to the inspection of any person or persons on request paying the clerk SIX-PENCE specie, and one shilling for a certified extract, as a fee: And if, after the establishment of this court, any person or persons shall be so hardy and daring as to decide any point of honor, contest or squabble, by duelling, or by appeals to the public in any of the public News-papers, or by hand-bills, it shall be deemed a contempt of the High Court of Honor, and the party or parties shall be rendered infamous, by having their name or names, respectively, entered in the RASCAL'S RECORD.

The process of the court shall be as follows: If any man has cause of offence against another, he shall apply to the clerk of the court for a DECLARATION: These declarations shall be fairly printed on a good paper with suitable blanks for the names of the parties, dates, &c. and shall be kept by the clerk of the court:

The party applying shall pay, to the clerk, EIGHTEEN PENCE for the blank and SIX PENCE for filling it up and attesting it, and the party shall sign the declaration with his own hand; after which the clerk shall number and file the said declaration. On certificate from the clerk, that such a declaration is filed, the judges shall meet and agree upon a time and place for the hearing; of which the accusers and accused shall have due notice to attend with their respective witnesses. No council shall be admitted in this court, but the parties must personally plead their own causes. After the hearing, the court shall give their final sentence: If judgment goes against the ACCUSEE, his name, &c. shall be registered in the RASCAL'S RECORD, with a number, in a column, for the purpose, referring to the number of the declaration filed; but if the accuser shall fail to make good and support his charge or charges against the accusee, his name shall be entered in the RASCAL'S RECORD, in place of the accusee: And thus shall all controversies be determined, where property is not concerned.

And the FORM of the DECLARATION shall be as follows, viz.

KNOW ALL MEN by these presents, That I, A. B. of the city of Philadelphia, do announce, pronounce, attest, publish and declare—That my friend and fellow-citizen, C. D. is a rogue, a rascal, a villain, a thief and scoundrel; that he is a murderer, a robber, a plunderer, a highwayman, a footpad and a cheat; that he has committed sacrilege, blasphemy, forgery, fornication, adultery, rape, sodomy and beastiality; that he is a tory, a traitor, a conspirator, a rebel and rioter; that he is a forestaller, a regrator, a monopolizer, a speculator and a depreciator; that he is a backbiter, a slanderer, a calumniator and a lier; that he is a mean, dirty, stinking, sniveling, sneaking, pimping, pocket-picking, d——d son of a bitch: And I do further declare that all and every of the above appellations are to be taken, received and construed in the most approbrious sense of the words.[1]

---

1. This echoes a letter in the *Packet*, 9 December, about Benjamin Rush, one of Dr. Shippen's supporters: "Dr. Rush is capable of LYING, in the worst SENSE of that approbrious WORD. . . ."

In testimony whereof I have hereunto set my hand, at Philadelphia aforesaid, this day of

NOW THE CONDITION of the above declaration is such, that if the aforesaid A. B. the accuser, shall and do, well and truly support, maintain and fully prove, before the judges of the High Court of Honor, any one or more of the aforesaid charges against his friend and fellow citizen, the said C. D. accusee, as aforesaid, then the said A. B. to be saved harmless, and remain justified in his proceedure: But, and if the accuser, aforesaid, shall fail to make proof as aforesaid, then he, the said A. B. doth submit, admit and permit, that his name, that is to say, the name of him the said A. B. accuser as aforesaid, shall be entered on the book of record of the said honorable court, called the RASCAL'S RECORD, there to be and remain, from generation to generation.

Signed and attested the day and year aforesaid.

Such, messrs. Printers, are the outlines of my scheme; which, I acknowledge, may admit of great improvement and enlargement. It would ill become me to expatiate on the many and great advantages that must accrue to my countrymen on such an establishment. How much bloodshed, how much inkshed will be spared; how many difficult points of honor and ceremony may be judicially determined; how many private animosities may be checked, in the first stage, by an appeal to the court of honour, before the blood gets heated by argument and altercation. These I leave to the judicious pens that will, doubtless, be employed in dissertations on the rights, limits, advantages, &c. of the HIGH COURT OF HONOR. I cannot, however, forbear pointing out one benefit that will arise from this scheme; which is, that when a person is so disposed, he may abuse and villify his friend or neighbour at a very reasonable charge, viz. the small sum of TWO SHILLINGS, specie; whereas it costs, the Lord knows what-all, to get a column or two of scandal and abuse into your paper: But modesty forbids me saying any more on this subject; I shall, therefore, silently wait the applauses of my fellow citizens.

CALAMUS.

*Pennsylvania Packet 23 December 1780.*

# IN A SCATOLOGICAL SEASON (1781-1782)

## RIVINGTON'S ADVERTISEMENT

On the 24th of October 1781, banner headlines in the *Freeman's Journal* of Philadelphia hailed the surrender of Cornwallis and "above 5000 British troops"—"Laus Deo–" Only slightly less restrained, other papers celebrated by printing and reprinting official dispatches from the front describing the surrender rites, and lively reports from out-of-town papers describing "illuminations" and festivities across the land. Buoyed by the national exuberance, Hopkinson poured forth a pair of hilarious satires on James Rivington, leading propagandist for the British and Loyalist establishment, who had too long depressed American spirits with false rumors, dire warnings, and awful prophecies. As the King's Printer of New York and publisher of the *Royal Gazette* there, Rivington made an obvious and easy target.

In England he had built a publishing empire on the works of Oliver Goldsmith, then gambled it away at the race course. Fleeing to Philadelphia in the mid-sixties, he had quickly built a new fortune with a chain of bookstores that also sold general merchandise. About 1765 he had moved on to New York, henceforth his headquarters. There, in 1773, he had founded a newspaper which, under a succession of names, gained national recognition for the quality of typography and catholicity of reporting. But his policy of giving all sides on an issue proved Rivington's undoing as the Tea Tax controversy boiled over. Patriots saw the slant of his stories intolerably un-American. Hauled before New York's powerful Whig Association in April 1775, he had pleaded freedom of the press, yet consented to print an apology. Nevertheless, a band of unsatisfied patriots from Connecticut raided his printshop and routed him out of the country.

Replenishing his presses and stocks in England, he had returned to a safer New York in October 1777, there to reissue his paper, first as

*America Triumphant and Britannia in Distress*

*Weatherwise's Town and Country Almanak, 1782, celebrates victory.*

the *Loyal Gazette* (which the patriots called, "the Lying Gazette") and then as the *Royal Gazette.* Under Crown patronage, he provided Continental papers with official British documents just as the *Pennsylvania Gazette* supplied them with official documents from Congress. He had further advantage in having direct access to American military secrets through British intelligence and Loyalist spies. Thoroughly skilled in propaganda, he had exploited this advantage to embarrass Washington and Congress, and perhaps delay American victory. While the British still held New York (until November 1783), he was still safe from retribution. But, as Hopkinson showed, he was not invulnerable to satire.

As Hopkinson found to his sorrow, Rivington was not without friends either, and they did not let the satires go unanswered. *Rivington's Gazette* overflowed with waves of scatology as Tory writers travestied an oratorio Hopkinson had written honoring Washington, then travestied his reply to their travesty, and a third time travestied his overture for an end to the skirmish. The rabid patriots who rushed to his defense in their own papers (matching the Tories' scatology) received his appeal for peace with outraged indignation, and redirected their attack to him until, as he had twenty years earlier, he sought his best defense in silence.

The first of the satires reprinted below pretends to be an advertisement copied from Rivington's newspaper, and the second his irate response to that spurious announcement.

## FROM THE NEW-YORK GAZETTE. ADVERTISEMENT

The late surrender of lord Cornwallis and his army must undoubtedly produce the most happy effects to the British nation, by accelerating the TERMINATION of the war and the views of the ministry with respect to America; as it will unavoidably interest foreign powers in behalf of the English, and has taken off a man who was inimical to the glory of sir Henry Clinton and perpetually counteracting his manœuvres.[1] In a word, *no one can*

1. Generals Clinton and Cornwallis were reportedly at odds in early 1781 because of a secret commission naming Cornwallis commander-in-chief to succeed Clinton. Tactically, the issue was that Clinton preferred to remain in New York instead of applying pressure on Virginia from the north as Cornwallis pacified the Carolinas.

*tell or foresee* the happy consequences of this important event. Nevertheless the subscriber finds it convenient, for *obvious reasons,* to remove to Europe. All persons therefore, who have any demands against, or are indebted to him, are requested to make a speedy settlement of their accounts. Notice is also hereby given, that the subscriber will dispose of his remaining stock in trade by public auction. The sale to begin at his store on Monday the 26th inst. and to continue from day to day (Sundays excepted) from the hours of ten to one in the forenoon, until the whole is disposed of. It is well known that his miscellaneous store consists of the most valuable and curious variety of articles that have ever been exhibited in this part of the world. The limits of an advertisement will by no means admit of an adequate display of this extraordinary collection; the subscriber will therefore content himself for the present with selecting a few articles for public attention—compleat catalogues will be given at the sale.

## BOOKS

The history of the American War: or the glorious exploits of generals GAGE, HOWE, BURGOYNE, CORNWALLIS, and CLINTON.

The Royal Pocket Companion; being a new system of policy, founded on rules deduced from the nature of man and approved by experience; whereby a prince may in a short time render himself abhorred by his subjects and detested by all good men.

A New and Complete System of Cruelty; containing a variety of modern improvements in that art, embellished with an elegant frontispiece, representing the inside view of a prison ship.

Select Fables of Æsop, with suitable morals and applications; amongst which are "The dog and the shadow," "The man and his goose which laid a golden egg," &c &c.

The right of Great Britain to the dominion of the sea.—A poetical fiction.

The State of Great Britain in October 1760, and October 1781, compared and contrasted.

A Geographical, Historical and Political History of the Rights and Possessions of the Crown of Great Britain in North America. This valuable work consisted of 13 vols in folio; but is abridged by a royal hand into a single pocket duodecimo, for the greater convenience of himself and his subjects.

The Law of Nations revised and amended; to which is added, by way of appendix, a *full & true* account of the capture of the island of St. Eustatia by admiral Rodney.[2]

A Full and True Account of the Conquest of the Four Southern Rebel Colonies; with notes critical and explanatory by earl Cornwallis.[3]

A Narrative of the Ship-wreck of lord Rawdon, in his voyage from Charlestown to London.[4]

Miracles not ceased; or the remarkable interposition of providence, in causing the moon to delay her setting for more than two hours, to favour the retreat of general Joshua and the British army, after the battle of Monmouth.[5]

The Political Lyar, a weekly paper published by the subscriber; bound in volumes.

---

2. After successes against the Spanish fleet, Admiral George Rodney sailed to engage the French fleet off the West Indies but was diverted when, capturing the undefended island of St. Eustatius, he found warehouses crammed with goods from English merchants destined for the American forces, and stayed three months plundering these goods as his own prize.
3. Starting his march through the Carolinas with 4000 men, Cornwallis reached the Virginia border with less than half that number, then in early March 1781, defeated General Greene at Guilford Court House, losing 500 more. Weakened by losses, fatigue, and short supplies, he fell back to Wilmington, virtually concluding the southern campaign.
4. Named Adjutant-General at 24 after heroic service, Francis Rawdon successfully aided Cornwallis in the Carolinas and was granted a leave to recover from exhaustion. Sailing to England in the summer of 1781, he was imprisoned when his ship was captured by a French cruiser.
5. Evacuating Philadelphia in 1778, General Clinton had elected to march to New York across 90 miles of enemy ground with a provision train 12 miles long. Harassed by Washington's guerrilla attacks, he had to stop and fight in oppressive mid-June heat, effecting his retreat only in the cool of the long night.

Tears of Repentance; or the present state of the loyal refugees in New-York and elsewhere.

## PLAYS

West Point Preserv'd; or the plot discovered. A tragi-comedy.

Miss McCrea—A tragedy.[6]

The Meschianza. A Pantomime.[7]

Burgoyne's Address. The Sleeveless Errand, or the commissioners of Peace. The March to Valley Forge. The Unsuccessful Attempt, by gov. Johnstone.[8] The Amorous Hero, and contented Cuckold, by gen. Howe.—Comedies.

The Battle of the Keggs. A farce.

Who'd Have Thought it, or the introduction of 24 British standards to the rebel congress. A procession.[9]

## MAPS AND PRINTS

An elegant Map of the British Empire in America, upon a *very small* scale.

An accurate Chart of the Coast of North America, from New Hampshire to Florida, with the soundings of all the principal

---

6. A widely publicized atrocity of July 1777 had been the shooting in cold blood of Miss Jane (Jenny) McCrea during an Indian-British attack on Fort Edwards, New York.
7. When General Clinton succeeded General Howe in May 1778 at Philadelphia, the officers tendered Howe a fantastic fete, the Meschianza, in which they dressed gaily as Persian knights and held a regatta on the river, as well as a glorious procession, a medieval tournament, and a gala ball.
8. Former governor of West Florida, George Johnstone was one of the three commissioners sent from England in June 1778 with terms of reconciliation, which Congress rejected. When Johnstone tried to bribe Joseph Reed, President of Pennsylvania, to exert his influence, Reed exposed the attempt with widespread publicity.
9. On 3 November, a week before this article appeared in the *Packet*, 24 regimental flags surrendered at Yorktown had been paraded down Market Street by French and American troops, then "laid at the feet" of Congress. (See note 18 *A Pretty Story*, p. 51 above.)

bays, harbours, rivers and inlets. This work was undertaken and completed by his majesty's special command, and at the national expence of many millions of money, thousands of men, and hundreds of royal ships and valuable merchantmen.

A Plan of Lord Cornwallis's Rout through the southern Colonies, beginning at Charlestown and terminating at Yorktown, in Virginia. As the preceding chart gives an accurate description of the sea coast, so it was intended to give a correct map of the internal parts of this country; but the savage inhabitants grew jealous of the operation, and actually prohibited his lordship's further progress.

A *very distant* Prospect of North America, neatly engraved.

A View of the Battle of Saratoga, and its companion the Siege of Yorktown.

British Representations of the principal Engagements in the present war, *highly coloured* by eminent hands. These pieces are so ingeniously contrived, that by reversing any one of them, it exhibits the American or French view of the same action *uncoloured.*

A humourous Representation of the triumphal Procession of brigadier general Arnold, and his friend & counsellor, through the streets of Philadelphia, in effigy.[10]

The Times: a satyrical print, representing the British lion as blind in both eyes, thirteen of his teeth drawn, and his claws pared off; with lord North, in the character of a farrier, bleeding him in the tail for his recovery.

## PHILOSOPHICAL APPARATUS

A curious new invented Magic Lanthorn, very useful for people at the head of affairs. This was constructed by an able artist

10. In September 1780, news of Arnold's treason reached Philadelphia, where he formerly served as military commander until removed for corruption. Search of his private papers then revealed widespread frauds, and an incensed citizenry paraded a cart carrying an effigy of Arnold in uniform with the devil shaking a purse at his ear.

under lord North's immediate direction, for the entertainment of the good people of England. The spectators are highly entertained with an illuminated view of the *fictitious* objects presented, but kept totally in the dark with respect to the *real* objects around them.

Multiplying Glasses, whereby the number of an enemy may be

---

*Benedict Arnold in Effigy*

***A two-faced Benedict Arnold paraded in effigy through Philadelphia contemplates the mask of treason before him and the devil behind.***

A REPRESENTATION of the FIGURES exhibited and paraded through the Streets of PHILADELPHIA, on *Sat*
the 30*th* of *September*, 1780.

*DESCRIPTION of the FIGURES.*

A STAGE raiſed on the body of a cart, on which was an effigy of General ARNOLD ſitting; this was dreſſed in regimentals, had two faces, emblematical of his traiterous conduct, a maſk in his left hand, and a letter in his right from Belzebub, telling him that he had done all the miſchief he could do, and now he muſt hang himſelf.

At the back of the General was a figure of the Devil, dreſſed in black robes, ſhaking a purſe of money at the general's left ear, and in his right hand a pitch-fork, ready to drive him into hell as the reward due for the many crimes which the thief of gold had made him commit.

In the front of the ſtage and before General Arnold, was placed a large lanthorn of tranſparent paper, with the conſequences of his crimes thus delineated, *i. e.* on one part, General Arnold on his knees before the Devil, who is pulling him into the flames—a label from the General's mouth with these words, "My dear Sir, I have ſerved you faithfully;" to which the Devil replies, "And I'll reward you." On another ſide, two ropes from a gallows, inſcribed, "The Traitors reward." And on the front of the lanthorn was wrote the following:

"MAJOR GENERAL BENEDICT ARNOLD, late COMMANDER of the FORT WEST-POINT. THE CRIME OF THIS MAN IS HIGH TREASON. "He has deſerted the important poſt WEST-POINT, on Hudſon's River, committed to his charge by His Excellency the Commander in Chief, and is gone off to the enemy at New-York.

"His deſign to have given up this fortreſs to our enemies, has been diſcovered by the goodneſs of the Omniſcient Creator, who has not only prevented his carrying it into execution, but has thrown into our hands ANDRE, the Adjutant-General of their army, who was detected in the character of a ſpy.

"The treachery of this ungrateful General is held up to public view, for the expoſition of infamy; and to proclaim with joyful acclamation, another inſtance of the interpoſition of bounteous Providence.

"The effigy of this ingrate is therefore hanged (for want of his body) as a Traitor to his native country, and a Betrayer of the laws of honour."

The proceſſion began about four o'clock, in the following order:

Several Gentlemen mounted on horſe-back.
A line of Continental Officers.
Sundry Gentlemen in a line.
A guard of the City Infantry.
Just before the cart, drums and fifes playing the Rogues March.
Guards on each ſide.

The proceſſion was attended with a numerous concourſe of people, who after expreſſing their abhorence of the Treaſon and the Traitor, committed him to the flames, and left both the effigy and the original to ſink into aſhes and oblivion.

'TWAS *Arnold's* POST ſir *Harry* ſough
*Arnold* ne'er enter'd in his thought,
How ends the bargain? let us ſee,
The fort is ſafe, as ſafe can be,
His favourite *per force* muſt die,
His view's laid bare to ev'ry eye;
His money's gone—and lo! he gains
One ſcoundrel more for all his pains.
ANDRE was *gen'rous*, *true*, and *brave*,
And in his room, he buys a knave.
'Tis ſure ordain'd, that *Arnold* cheats
All thoſe, of courſe, with whom he treats.
Now let the *Devil* ſuſpect a bite
Or *Arnold* cheats him of his right.

*Mothers ſhall ſtill their children, and say---*Arnold!--
*Arnold ſhall be the bug-bear of their years.*
*Arnold!---vile, treacherous, and leagued with Satan.*

greatly increased, to cover the disgrace of a defeat, or enhance the glory of a victory.

Microscopes, for magnifying small objects, with select setts of objects ready fitted—amongst which are a great variety of real and supposed successes of the British arms in America.

A complete Electrical Apparatus, with improvements, for the use of the king and his ministers. This machine should be used with great caution, otherwise, as unhappy experience hath shown, the operator may unexpectedly *receive* the shock he intended to *give.*

Pocket Glasses for near sighted politicians, &c. &c. &c.

## PATENT MEDICINES

Aurum Potabile. This preparation was formerly deemed a never-failing medicine in all cases; but was thought not so well adapted to the American climate, having been frequently tried here without effect; but its reputation is now restored, having been administered with great success in the case of general Arnold.

Vivifying Balsam, excellent against weak nerves, palpitations of the heart, over bashfulness and diffidence; in great demand for the use of the army.

Sp. Mend. or, The true Spirit of Lying, extracted by a distillation of some hundreds of the ROYAL GAZETTE OF NEW-YORK. Other papers have been tried, but it is found, after much experience, that there is a peculiar quality in the component parts of the paper and ink of the Royal Gazette, which alone can produce this spirit in true perfection. By administering due proportions of this medicine, lies may be formed which are to operate for a week, a month or months; [near] at hand or at a distance, in America or Europe.

N.B. Directions, drawn up by the subscriber, will be given with each bottle.

Cordial Drops for low spirits, prepared for the use of the Board of Loyal Refugees at New-York.

Anodyne Elixir, for quieting fears and apprehensions, very necessary for Tories in all parts of America.

With a great variety of articles too tedious to mention.

N.B. To every purchaser to the Value of £5 will be given *gratis* one quire of counterfeited continental currency, also two quires of proclamations, offering pardon to the rebels. Printed on soft paper.

JAMES RIVINGTON

*Freeman's Journal 21 November 1781, reprinted from Pennsylvania Packet 10 November 1781.*

## *RIVINGTON'S REPLY*

Ultimately the model for both the "Advertisement" and the "Reply" that followed in next week's *Packet* was Swift's "Partridge Papers," in which Partridge the astrologer is declared dead and then objects that he is very much alive. Closer to Hopkinson's own time were two satires by his old friend President John Witherspoon of Princeton. Witherspoon's "Recantation of Benjamin Towne" in the *New-York Packet* for 1 October 1778 had made that Tory printer confess, recant, and apologize to the nation: "An incredible lie can obtain no belief and therefore at least must be perfectly harmless. . . ." The pseudo-"Towne" then went on to argue that the most effective way to disgrace any cause is to publish mountains of monstrous lies in its favor.

Even more recently, Witherspoon had written a parody for the *United States Magazine* (January 1779), "The Humble Representation and earnest Supplication of James Rivington." Here the pseudo-"Rivington" offers to barter with Congress—their mercy in exchange for his talents as a pimp for military officers and a liar for the newspapers. In another exercise in sophistry, he argues that his notoriety should be no bar to success: "I might by doubling the deception, and writing those things only, or chiefly, which you would wish to be disbelieved, render you the most essential service" (1:40). Besides maintaining Witherspoon's strategy and tone, Hopkinson also followed him in parodying Rivington's Latinate style. The essential difference, however, is that Witherspoon's essays slipped into sarcasm, while Hopkinson's sustains the straight-faced irony of the "Advertisement."

Sir,

Your Paper of the 10th Inst. No. 805, reached this city, and an advertisement there inserted and signed with my signature has attracted particular notice, and rendered me the object of much satirical stricture. The author of this wicked forgery, whoever he is, has most nefariously and with malice aforethought, made use of my name to impose on the public the nugatory productions of his own flimsy brain, as the genuine offspring of my prolific pen. But I do assure you, upon the word of a gentleman, that said advertisement is, *in toto,* fictitious and spurious. Was the *ultimatum* of this *jejune* performance nothing more than risible satire, I could suffer the indignity with taciturn patience: but it is most patent to sense that an emphatic injury is intended by this atrocious calumniator. The manifest design is to draw upon me the resentment of a people for whom I have the most profound veneration, and whose virtuous and heroic struggles for constitutional liberty I have beheld with astonishment and secret admiration.

You may perhaps, Mr. Claypoole,[1] be surprized at this manifesto, and exclaim that there is no concatenation between such a declaration and the general tendency of the Royal Gazette of New-York. In answer to this, you are to consider that it was my lot to remain with a people who had power in their hands and money in their purses. In this situation it was the part of a wise man to evade the power and possess as much of the money as possible. This I have endeavoured to do. I have wrote and published for them as far as invention could go; the English language has been tortured and truth expired on the rack in their behalf. By this I have gained their confidence and blinded the jealous eye of power. As to their money, let the baubles I have sold them at extortionate prices, and the salary I enjoy, evince that my labour hath not been in vain. Have I done this to the injury of

1. To allow himself more freedom for his interests in the militia and philanthropy, John Dunlap had elevated his apprentice David Claypoole to partnership in the *Packet.*

America and the advantage of her enemies? By no means—By overacting my part I defeated the purpose I seemed to have in view, and the political lies I daily fabricated only served to gull the fools, who believed I was exerting myself in their service. In a word, my paper had no credit but in the cities of London and New York. As to the cash I have seduced from the unbutton'd pockets of cockaded coxcombs, I hope to spend it in America, the land of liberty, when the storm of war shall cease, and every man shall enjoy the fruits of his ingenuity under his own vine and his own fig tree.

I am well persuaded, Mr. Claypoole, that the voice of your multitude is against me. They judge from appearances only; and appearances are generally delusive. They suppose I am the sole author of all the inveterate falsehoods and misrepresentations which I so frequently publish. Alas! alas! *I am but a poor printer,* subjected, by my vocation, to the disagreeable task of bringing into the world the monstrous conceptions of disordered fancies.—But I am deemed a tory—a malevolent tory—why?—because I have published tory news, tory lies and tory essays in my gazette —granted.—But will any one pretend to say that I have refused to publish whig news, whig lies or whig essays? I challenge all Philadelphia to produce a single writer who ever sent me a whig piece for publication, which I refused or neglected to print. I am confident no such instance can be found. The truth is, I am a friend to liberty, and have actually felt the sacred flame kindle in my breast. First about the time, or at least just after, the affair of Saratoga; and now again on the surrender of lord Cornwallis and his army; and if the brave Americans should pursue their success and confirm their independence, of which indeed there remains little doubt, you may depend upon it there is not a flaming patriot in the thirteen united states that will sing forth the charms of liberty with more loquaceous zeal than myself.

It is the duty of every man to serve his king and country. I am desirous of fulfilling this duty to the point of punctuality. I have already served my king, my sovereign George the IIId. God bless him!—to the best of my abilities; and now I am ready to wheel to the right about and serve my country. For I call this my country wherein I have eaten the bread of luxury, and risen to an height of importance and opulence which I had no hopes of obtaining in England, that land of debts, creditors and intolerable oppression. Finally, Mr. Claypoole, I rest the evidence of my whiggism on two immoveable pillars. First, the declaration I voluntarily signed and which was published in the news-papers of the year 1776,[2] wherein I asserted my attachment to the American cause, and solemnly engaged to do nothing against it; and, secondly, my address to Congress lately forwarded by *Mr. John Moody;*[3] a copy of which I subjoin for your satisfaction.

"To the Honourable the CONGRESS of the *United States of America.*

"The PETITION of *James Rivington* of the City of New York, Printer and Nick-nack Seller, Humbly sheweth:

"That your Petitioner, under the sacred influence of the most exalted ideas of the glorious cause of liberty, for which you have so nobly, so wisely, and so effectually contended, begs leave, with all due submission, to throw himself at the feet of the most venerable, most august body on the face of the earth.

"That your Petitioner hath, from a most unfortunate arrangement of circumstances been compelled, most unwillingly, not only to remain with the enemies of your virtuous cause, but even to assist them to the utmost of his power. But he begs leave most solemnly to assure your honours, that he hath done this with the utmost compunction and sorrow of heart; and hath been often known to exclaim, *in private,* with the royal psalmist—*Woe is me, that I am constrained to dwell with Mesech and to have my habitation among the tents of Kedar.*—

"That your Petitioner, having given undeniable proofs of his

2. In the *Gazette,* 4 May 1775, forced to apologize for slanting the news, Rivington had written: "Nothing which I have done, has proceeded from any sentiments in the least unfriendly to the Liberties of this Continent," and that he would avoid giving further "Offence to the inhabitants of the Colonies. . . ."

3. Brother of the more notorious spy, James Moody, John was executed 13 November 1781 for trying to burglarize the Pennsylvania State House and carry off the secret journals of Congress to New York.

abilities in the art of political deviation from truth, in support of a *bad cause,* humbly conceives, that the same talents may be of singular service in defending a *good one;* and therefore offers himself, with all his rare and useful accomplishments, to the Congress of the *free and united States of America;* only praying such protection and such reward as his future services may justly entitle him to.

"That your Petitioner hath frequently declared, that if he had been *properly* engaged on the *right side,* he would long since have written the United States into a confirmed independence; and have abandon'd the *wrong side* to the disappointment its partizans so justly merit.

"Submitting the premises to your candid consideration, he only waits your favourable answer to appear a first-rate whig in the city of Philadelphia. And, in the mean time has the honour to subscribe himself, with all due respect."—&c. &c. &c.

Such, Mr. Claypoole, is my address to Congress. I have now only to request of you, that you will not admit into your paper, any more of the false and wicked insinuations of the author of the aforesaid Advertisement. I promise myself an agreeable answer from Congress, and hope *Mr. Thomson*[4] will not be dilatory in forwarding it. Soon after which, I expect to take you by the hand, and salute you with the endearing names of Brother Puff and Brother Whig. 'Till then, allow me to be

Your esteemed friend,
and humble servant,

J. RIVINGTON

New-York,
Nov. 17, 1781.
*Pennsylvania Packet 20 November 1781.*

---

4. Charles Thomson, who served as secretary of Congress, was also head of the secret service. He was later alleged to have been employing Rivington as one of his agents. See J. Thomas Scharf & Thompson Westcott, *History of Philadelphia* (Philadelphia, 1884), 1:275.

# *PARODY ON A SCENE FROM* MACBETH

Rivington did not reply to Hopkinson's "Advertisement" or "Reply" but soon evened the score with a blow at Hopkinson's reputation as a composer and occasional poet. Worse, he used him as a stalking horse for an attack on Washington and the French allies: Commissioned by the French minister, Hopkinson composed an "oratorial entertainment" for a fete honoring General Washington the evening of 11 December 1781, and called it, fittingly, "The Temple of Minerva" after the goddess of wisdom. The *Royal Gazette* reviewed it three weeks later by printing a scatological parody, "The Temple of Cloacina," so named in honor of the goddess of sewage.

Before Hopkinson could manage a reply to that one, a Philadelphia newspaper, the *Freeman's Journal,* rose in patriotic wrath to defend him from Rivington's Tory barbs. Its editor Philip Freneau adored General Washington this side of idolatry, and hated the enemy with raw passion. Other newspapers had praised the fall of Cornwallis as a victory for the allied troops, but not Freneau. He thanked God and urged Americans to compound divine favor with human vengeance. Furthermore, he seldom missed the chance to ridicule Rivington as a born loser, so his defense of Hopkinson was wholly in character.

Freneau claimed that the "Temple of Cloacina" was the nefarious work of a Tory parson, once Hopkinson's dear friend—"that wolf in sheep's clothing, parson Odell" (13 January, 1782). He challenged Odell and Rivington to a sewage-slinging contest, which the *New York Gazette* eagerly joined—especially when Hopkinson himself wrote a tepid reply of his own, telling how he had looked in vain all over Philadelphia for a copy of Rivington's newspaper, only to find the sole sample floating down the communal sewer. The *Gazette* thereupon pretended to reprint Hopkinson's little story as "A true and faithful NARRATIVE of the ADVENTURE of a poor unfortunate *Poet* and *Musician,* in his Search after Rivington's ROYAL GAZETTE in the City of Philadelphia." The piece was subtitled, "The *second* Edition with Additions and Emendations," but, except for its opening paragraph and an occasional verbatim excerpt, it was another travesty, more scatological than the previous one.

Hopkinson's reaction to this latest travesty contrasted remarkably with his reply to "Cloacina." In the *Packet* for 9 February, he published an open letter, "To the AUTHOR of two Columns and an half in Rivington's Gazette, of the 26th of January," refusing to pursue the contest. The laws of literary warfare did not require him to follow his antagonist "into all the filth hè is willing to wade through." But Hopkinson insists that his reasons for breaking off the present exchange are his respect and friendship for the anonymous attacker: "*A sense of gratitude for former favours, and a still subsisting friendship on my part,* render the combat altogether unequal. If you have not conducted yourself according to my opinion of what is right and honourable, I can only be sorry for it, and regret, that you have not employed the eminent abilities, I know you possess, in a manner more worthy yourself and them." Moreover, Hopkinson vows to maintain his attacker's anonymity in private as well as public, then—as if to show he harbors no hard feelings—wipes his pen, "not with an handful of shavings—but with a piece of clean cotton" and lays it by.

(Hopkinson's secret was well kept, for even today the identity of his antagonist who signed himself "M. G." is a matter for mere speculation.[1] My own candidate is a medical gentleman, Abraham Chovet, an eccentric Philadelphia physician whose skill in the healing arts was so effective that he dwelt unmolested in the city even though a loud, brazen supporter of Loyalty and Loyalists. Notorious for profanity so habitual that it had become an unconscious part of his speech, he also built a reputation for telling jokes about the Americans and their French allies, even at the French Minister's table.[2] At the same time, he could be vicious in wit combat, a fault his friends saw fit to endure because of his otherwise eminent abilities and generosity. Hopkinson, now afflicted with gout, could easily have been grateful to him for past favors, and would not have been alone in feeling friendship for the eccentric old doctor despite his scurrilous behavior.)

But in refusing to identify his antagonist, Hopkinson had lent some weight to the *Freeman Journal's* allegation that the "Temple of Cloacina" had been written by "that wolf in sheep's clothing, parson Odell." In the *Journal* of 20 February, then, he published a demurrer from Odell along with a note of his own protesting the calumny. The *Journal* replied with the same allegation, then attacked Hopkinson for denying it and taking the part of "one of the most bitter enemies to your country." The attack concluded with a heavy-handed warning: "Such professions ill become a gentleman in public office, and may make

1. Lewis Leary, "Francis Hopkinson, Jonathan Odell, and 'The Temple of Cloacina': 1782," *AL,* 15 (1943), 183–91.
2. James L. Whitehead, ed., "The Autobiography of Stephen Du Ponceau," *PMHB,* 63 (1939), 326–28.

many suspect that your 'friendship' extends farther than 'a sense of gratitude for former favours' ought to lead it" (6 March).

Stung by the aspersion cast upon his patriotism, Hopkinson reacted in the *Packet* for 2 April, assuming the role of a hack writer applying for a place on the *Freeman's Journal,* and submitting as a sample of his work a parody of a witches scene from *Macbeth;* the burden of the parody is that the *Journal's* ink is compounded of gangrenous slime and bitter gall.

## *A PARODY ON A SCENE IN* MACBETH

*Scene, a blind Alley:*
*Enter three Scriblers.*

1st Sc. When shall we three meet again
To vex the heart and wreck the brain?

2nd Sc. When the mid-night moon invites,
When the howling cur affrights,
Then we'll hold our magic rites.

3rd Sc. Where the place?

2nd Sc. —In garret high;
Above the earth, beneath the sky;
We'll the infernal ink prepare,
Fraught with mischief, discord, care;

1st & 3d Sc. We'll not fail to meet you there.

Exeunt.

*Scene a Garret: a large Pot of Printer's*
*Ink standing on the Floor.*
*Enter the Three Scriblers.*

1st Sc. Where hast thou been?

3rd Sc. —Hearing Tales;
Private slander much prevails.

1st Sc. Brother, where thou!

2nd Sc. With the noisy croud to sue

For a place I had in view.
Avaunt thee wretch! a sullen patriot cries;
Avaunt! the people thy request denies.
Revenge! Revenge for this I'll take;
Haste the infernal ink to make.
Tho' their cause cannot be lost,
Yet, it shall be vex'd and crost.
Seeds of discord we will sow;
Seeds that never fail to grow.
Dire dissention, envy, hate
Shall not fail to propagate.
Num'rous shall their offspring be;
Scorpion-tongued—Hell's progeny.
Fair is foul, and foul is fair;
Haste! th' infernal ink prepare.

1st Sc. Look what I've got—a hero's name—
2nd Sc. Oh, blast his fame!

3rd Sc. —Blast his fame!
2nd Sc. And I, a senator's profound
For wisdom, prudence, truth renown'd.
3rd Sc. His deeds to infamy we'll turn all,
And murder in the *Freeman's Journal*. . . .

*Pennsylvania Packet 2 April 1782.*

# *WRITINGS FOR THE POSTWAR PRESS* (1782-1787)

The real force behind the *Freeman's Journal* attack on Hopkinson was a concurrent struggle for control of the Pennsylvania Assembly. He was a leader of the new Republican Society, a signer of its manifesto calling for revision of the state constitution of 1776 which vested all power, including judicial and executive appointments, in that legislature. The Republicans urged democratic reforms, checks and balances, while the Constitutionalists, entrenched in the Assembly, jealously sought to preserve their oligarchic power. Organ of the Constitutionalists since its inception, the *Freeman's Journal* rumbled loudly against any revision as subversion. Slinging aspersions at Hopkinson's patriotism, a writer signing himself "Hater of Sycophants" made sure that readers recalled Hopkinson's signature on the Republican manifesto when it attacked "the people of Pennsylvania for daring to uphold the *constitution*" (10 April 1782). Only after the Republicans won the Assembly in the election of November 1782 did the *Freeman's Journal* soften its tone. Thereafter, Hopkinson would contribute to its columns as though the previous winter's feuding had been merely a domestic scrap.

Celebrating the Republican victory, he composed but did not publish a humorous allegorical tale about a struggle for power in the household of the Lady Pensylva, recently widowed by the death of her husband, Patriotism, just as she was about to bear a son, Independence. Imitating Fielding's style in *Tom Jones,* Hopkinson peopled his tale with caricatures of figures from both Republican and Constitutionalist camps—including "Fanny Belly" for Francis Bailey, proprietor of the *Freeman's Journal.* But during the next few years, he reserved such personal satire for his private notebooks, vowing to avoid what his mentor, Benjamin Franklin, described as "Pieces of Personal Abuse"[1]—pieces so scandalous that Franklin screened American newspapers before showing them to curious readers abroad.

This is not to say that Hopkinson abandoned political satire. He shifted his sights from state to local politics where the target remained the same; for the all-powerful assembly also controlled the municipal government of Philadelphia. The city's proprietary charter had dissolved in 1776 and no charter would replace it until 1789. Until then, both government and municipal services were functions of assembly committees or their appointees. Thus when Hopkinson criticized local ordinances or services, one eye was squinting at the state legislature. When the assembly ordered trees removed from city streets, he published an oration by a wooden post lamenting the blow to the ecology. An aroused public forced the assembly to repeal the ordinance at the height of a fierce election campaign.

Sometime during the winter of 1782, Hopkinson recopied into two notebooks all his satires he thought worth saving, omitting the scatological and concluding with the speech of the post as though that were to be his last word. But he went on composing new work, and during 1783 commented on such popular issues as the safest location for Congress (Why not equip it with wheels for easier transport?). The next year, he returned to promoting a better quality of urban life with a Lucianic dialogue between a dog and a cat left dead in the gutter, waiting for the city street cleaners to dispose of them. Except for a veiled attack on the political opposition leadership in an essay on portrait painting, he maintained his vow to abjure personal satire.

## *THE POST'S ORATION*

On 15 April 1782 the assembly passed a twelve-part act regulating the construction of walls or fences and otherwise providing for improvements in Philadelphia streets and highways. Provisions were included for removing derelict buildings and also for removing all the trees in the city because they had been obstructing "passage and prospect," plugging water courses, and uprooting pavements. In case of fire they could contribute to conflagration or at least impede the fire engines. Property owners were given six months to remove the

1. A. H. Smyth, ed., *Writings* (New York, 1905–07), 8:647.

trees or face fines. But a little over six months later (20 September) the assembly repealed this provision of the act because "a considerable Number of the Inhabitants of the City of *Philadelphia* have by their Petition set forth, that Trees planted in the Streets thereof conduce much to the Health of the Inhabitants, and are in other Respects of great Utility."[1] The language of the petition echoed Hopkinson's essay in the *Pennsylvania Gazette* for 21 August in which he created an eloquent wooden post to plead the case for all tree-kind.

This is a marvelously well-read post, familiar with science fiction as well as the Bible and knowledgeable about latest findings in botany. He cites authorities from the celebrated John Ray to the obscure Samuel Morland, and alludes to a recent (1779) work by Jan Ingen Housz, Dutch physician resident in London, announcing the discovery of photosynthesis and explaining how trees support animal life by manufacturing oxygen from carbon dioxide (i.e., beneficial from noxious gasses). He has also read widely among the moral philosophers, such as the Americans Samuel Johnson and Cadwallader Colden and British writers from John Locke to David Hume. He can thus plead from moral grounds as well as from the necessity of public health.

Gentlemen,

Looking over a file of papers which lay on my table, I found a very extraordinary speech, delivered by a very extraordinary personage in the House of Assembly in April last; which I had taken down in short hand; but not from the *mouth* of the speaker. I much wonder that this oration, with the surprising circumstances that attended it, hath not been handed to you before now. I hope you will rescue it from oblivion, by allowing it a place in your paper.

On the 12th of April last the House took up, for a third reading, and was debating by paragraphs a bill, intituled "An act for regulating party walls and partition fences in the city of Philadelphia," &c. &c. when, to the amazement of all present, the business was interrupted by a voice, perfectly articulate, proceeding from the capital of one of the columns which support the ceiling of the room. This voice claimed a right to be heard on the sub-

1. *Laws, Enacted in Third Sitting of Sixth General Assembly* (Philadelphia, 1783), Ch. XXXV.

ject of the bill then in debate. After the first astonishment at such an unusual prodigy had a little subsided, the right of a column to interfere in the business of the House was considered and objected to. And it was urged, that no instance had ever occured where a *wooden* member, a *block*-head, had presumed to speak in that House: That this column could by no construction of law be admitted as the representative of any part or district of Pennsylvania, having never been balloted for, elected, or returned by any officer of government as a member of Assembly: That the House when fully met must necessarily consist of a certain number of members *and no more,* and that this number is full and complete by the returns from the several counties, as appears by the records of the House; therefore, if this column should be allowed a voice, there must be a supernumerary member some where, which would be a violation of law and the constitution: And, lastly, that it was contrary to the order of nature that an *inanimate log* should presume to interfere in the affairs of *rational* beings; Providence having been pleased to distinguish so obviously between *men* and *things.*

To all this the column *firmly* replied, That he was properly a *standing member* of that *House,* having been duly *fixed* in his station by those who had the power and right to *place* him there: That he was the true representative of a numerous race, descended in a direct line from the *aborigines* of this country; those venerable ancestors who gave the name of Penn's-*sylvania* to this State, and whose numerous posterity now inhabit every county in it: That he was not only a member of the House, but one of its *principal supporters,* in as much as they could never *make a House* without him: That he had faithfully attended the public business, having never been fined as an absentee, and that those very members who were now opposing him had confided in his wisdom and integrity by appealing[2] to him in every contest respecting the rules and internal œconomy of the House: And

2. *The Rules of the House are hung up against one of the columns.* [Hopkinson's note.]

lastly, That as the bill under consideration so nearly concerned his fellow creatures, and he found himself miraculously endowed with speech, as if given for the occasion, he was determined to use his present power in behalf of those who could not speak for themselves.—After much debate, it was resolved that the House would hear what this importunate column had to say respecting the bill before them, but peremptorily refused him a vote on this or any other business in that Assembly.

The Columnar Orator having obtained leave, addressed the House in the following words:

"I am happy, Oh fellow citizens, that speech hath been allowed me on so important an occasion. I *stand* here this day an *upright* advocate for injured innocence. What fury, what madness, Oh deluded senators, hath induced you to propose the extirpation of those to whom you are indebted for so many of the elegancies, comforts and blessings of life? If the voice of justice is not to be regarded within these walls, let at least your own interests influence you to what is right; for I hope to shew that your safety and happiness are much more deeply concerned in the business you are upon, than you are at present aware of.

By the 12th section of the bill before you it is proposed to cut down and remove all the trees standing in any of the streets, lanes or alleys of this city.—What? Do we hold our lives on such uncertain tenure? Shall the inoffensive and respectable inhabitants of this city *stand* or *fall* by the caprice of a few ignorant petitioners? And will this House without remorse give their sanction to an edict which hath not had a parallel since the sanguinary days of *Herod* of Jury?[3] But I hope to convince this honorable House, that trees, as well as men, are capable of enjoying the rights of citizenship, and therefore ought to be protected in those rights; that having committed no offence, this arbitrary edict ought not to pass against them, and that your own welfare is nearly concerned in their culture and preservation.

3. According to Matthew 2:16, Herod of Judea ordered the massacre of all children in Bethlehem.

The superiority which man hath assumed over what he calls the *irrational* and *inanimate* creation, is a superiority only founded in their own pride and ignorance of our nature and faculties. The same divine hand that formed you, formed us also; the same elements that nourish you, nourish us also; like you we are composed of bones, blood-vessels, fibres and, for ought you know, nerves and muscles; witness the whole class of sensitive plants, wherein voluntary motion is manifest even to your eyes; like you we flourish in health or languish with disease; like you we die and return to the earth from which we sprang; and then, the wisest amongst you cannot distinguish between the dust of an *elm* and an *Emperor*. But I go much farther, and assert from your own authorities that we sleep and wake; that we are male and female; that we are married and given in marriage, and propagate our species to fuller effect and in nearly the same manner that you do. In support of this I could cite many respectable authorities from the ancients, and amongst the moderns *Grew, Millington, Ray, Camerarius, Morland, Geoffroy, Vaillant,* and, above all, your favourite *Linnaeus*.[4] Wherein then doth the vast difference between man and the vegetable world consist? I am bold to ask, wherein doth it consist?—Oh, cries yonder loquacious Lord of the creation, we can *converse;* we can *reason.* —Oh, cries yonder restless and fidgetty member, we can *move* from place to place.—To the latter, I answer, so can a beast, a fish, a bird, and to much better advantage than he can, with all his *locomotive* faculties—the former requires a more serious reply.—We can *converse,* we can *reason*—be it so—man, arbitrary man, hath affixed certain ideas to certain noises or sounds, if these sounds are adapted to his miserable apprehension, they are called language, reason, music and what not? But if the man should not be wise enough to understand the meaning of the noise he hears, he hesitates not to stile it jargon, nonsense, un-

4. Nehemiah Grew (1641–1705), Rudolf Jakob Camerarius (1665–1721), Samuel Morland (1663–1716), Etienne-François Geoffroy (1672–1731), Sébastian Vaillant (1669–1722); and Charles Linnaeus (1707–1778).

intelligible stuff. Thus, *a man* stands up and makes a long noise, called *Philosophy, Divinity, Law &c. An ass* lifts up his head and makes a much greater noise, and it is called *braying*. Yet, to his own species, the ass is an intelligent creature, and his language is well understood by them. If then man can thus mistake the matter with respect to brutes, although he sees that nature hath given them the organs of speech, and daily hears them exercise those organs for the purposes intended, how much more may he be mistaken as to the language of plants; a language too refined to make any impression on his gross and callous senses. That such a language doth actually exist, might be sufficiently proved from Scripture where we are repeatedly told that the valleys rejoice and sing, and the cedars of Lebanus praise the Lord: But I shall content myself with reading to your Honors a passage to this purpose from that ingenious author *Cyrano de Bergerac*—Voyage to the Moon, page 91.—"This fancy of eating by himself made me curious to know the reason of it: I was answered, that he chose not to taste either the odor of meats or of herbs, unless they had died spontaneously, because he imagined them beings capable of grief. I am not much surprised, replied I, that some orders of people here abstain from flesh and things that have sensitive life, yet it seems to me ridiculous to fear hurting a cabbage in the cutting. For my part, replied the Demon, I must own there appears to me good reasons for such an opinion; for is not a cabbage a being existing in nature as you are? have you not both her equally for your mother? and she is more immediately so to the vegetal than the rational production. The generation of the latter she hath left to the whim of a parent, a rigor she doth not extend to the former, in as much as she *obliges* one to produce another; and whilst one man is scarcely able to get more than a score of his species at best, a head of cabbage shall produce four or five hundred of its own sort. Should we say that nature hath a greater esteem for a man than she has for a cabbage, it would be only with a view to make us laugh; for nature is incapable of passion, and can neither love nor hate. If she was susceptible of love, she certainly would have a greater tenderness for the inoffensive cabbage than for the unrelenting man who destroys it—and again page 95, who has given us the knowledge of certain beings superior to us? to whom we are neither related nor proportioned, and whose existence we find it as difficult to conceive as the manner in which a cabbage can address itself to its own species. To understand which communication, our senses are too weak.—Remember, if you can, amongst all the species of animals, one more proud than the cabbage; who while you destroy him, is above complaining; yet though he disdains to murmur, he thinks nevertheless the more: If he wants such organs as you are master of, formed for wailings and tears, yet he has others, wherewith to implore heaven to revenge the injury done him; and expects it will not be with-held. It is not unlikely but you may ask how I know the cabbage has these fine thoughts? But inform me first, can you prove it has not? Or that at the close of the night, the Russia cabbage does not say to the Savoy, *Good Savoy, your most humble servant.*"[5]

But still, says man, we have *rationality* and *risibility* to distinguish us from the rest of the creation. That is, when nature gave one man the power to *reason,* she gave another the power to *laugh* at him. For our parts we are contented to be directed by the laws of nature, which fully enables us to answer the end of our creation; we pretend not to be wiser than the hand that made us and therefore we are guilty of no follies or excesses: We employ none of our powers in devising means for the more speedy and effectual destruction of our species: we do all the good we can, and, when we can do no more, retire from existence to make room for our successors. This rationality, on which you so much value yourselves, is, in my opinion, a striking mark of imbecility and disgrace; a punishment inflicted upon your race, doubtless, for some heinous offence, heretofore committed. The intelligent beings of the spiritual world never *reason;* they see truth intuitively; they know the whole chain of causes and effects; they see that in a triangle the greatest angle must be sub-

5. Translated by Samuel Derrick (London, 1754).

tended by the longest side without reasoning upon the case; and in terrestrial nature there is no creature but man that is obliged to *reason;* they all perform their respective functions with certainty and precision, under the directions of a law which cannot err; whilst your *reason* is ever involving you in absurdities and difficulties; is ever deducing false conclusions from false premises; and the wiser you think yourselves the more mischief you do. What is reason one day is not reason another. About 30 years ago you *reasoned* upon the disease called the *small-pox,* and thousands in every city and country fell sacrifices to your *rational* system; but you have now discovered that your system is no longer *rational,* and have adopted a different mode of practice;[6] this has been the case in almost every art and science. Besides this, your reason teaches you to square all nature by your ideas of truth—and you know not what truth is. For instance you eat and drink and walk, and you say I have *life;* but yonder *willow* can do none of these, therefore, it is *inanimate.* Deluded man! can your weak intellects discover all the nice gradations of life from the stone to the moss that adheres to it; from the moss to the sensative plant to the oyster; from the oyster to the ape; from the ape to the man; from the man to the angel; from the angel to an infinite series of beings, whom you know nothing of? Do you not see that all the exhibitions in nature are but different modifications and degrees of the same original essence or principle? Is not the gravity which retains *Jupiter* in his orbit, the same gravity which operates on a grain in the scales of a Jew?—The intelligent beings above you amuse themselves with the ridiculous blunders your *rationality* is continually making. They despise the wretch who stretches every faculty of his mind to amass a hoard of wealth, which he has not the spirit to enjoy; they pity the inevitable fate of the voluptuous and the vain toils of ambition, but they laugh incessantly at the folly of him who ransacks

---

6. From its introduction at Boston in 1721, inoculation against smallpox faced violent opposition on religious grounds, but by 1777 it had proven so effective that Washington ordered the entire Army inoculated.

the earth to gather sticks and stones, shells and bones, and, after spending years in arranging them, makes a *rareeshow* of his collection, and struts a *philosopher,* full of self importance and vain conceit.—If folly were the only effect of your reason, it might be patiently born with, but when you exercise it to over-reach, deceive, ruin and destroy each other; when you exert it's powers to conceal or embarrass truth, to establish falshood, to lead the blind out of his way and the lame into a ditch; to render yourselves more ingeniously wicked, and more effectually mischievous; these divine intelligences look with horror on you and your boasted reason; they turn aside from the hateful object, and view with pleasure the stately oak and wide spreading beach, the water loving willow and the fruitful vine, even all the vegetable creation, which, from the pine that waves on the mountain top to the herb that drinks the dew of the valley, fill with exact propriety their respective stations, and are invariably governed by the laws of nature, which are the laws of wisdom.—After all, your reason is but instinct broke loose; or rather, instinct is reason confined within proper bounds, and directed to the proper objects. Do not then presume upon a faculty, which upon the whole will be found to have been the curse of your species. To prove this you need only look into history for the facts and characters of former times, or to look round you for those of the present.

I might now, may it please your honors, point out many circumstances, wherein nature hath most evidently and advantageously distinguished the brutal and vegetable creation from man, by a real and substantial superiority: But lest I should wander too far in so large a field, and encroach upon your patience, I shall confine myself to one instance only. When a man dies, when he can no longer perform any of the functions of life, his body in a few hours becomes a useless, loathsome mass of corruption, which his nearest friends hurry away, and put out of sight forever. It is not so with us. Witness my appearance here this day. It is now some years since an end was put to my vegetal life by the fatal axe; my skin was stripped off and my limbs lopped away; yet you see my body is still of use; I stand here *firm, sound* and *hearty;* and, barring an accident from all consuming fire, I shall attend the future debates in this House, when all those, whom I have now the honor to address, *shall be no more.*

Having, I hope, fully convinced your honors that trees as well as men are capable of citizenship, I shall now proceed to consider the crimes and offences with which the trees of this city have been charged, and which the 12th section of the bill before the House is intended to punish.

The preamble to this section sets forth: "Whereas trees growing in the public streets, lanes and alleys of the said city of Philadelphia, do obstruct the prospect and passage through the same, and also disturb and disorder the water-courses and footways by the extending and encrease of the roots thereof, and must tend to spread fires when any break out within the said city: *Be it therefore enacted" &c. &c.*

Your honors have an old saying, called a proverb, which naturally occurs on this occasion—*It is easy to find a stick to beat a dog*—That is, a man is never at a loss for a reason for punishing those that are in his power, and whom he wishes to oppress—But these trees, it seems, obstruct the prospect; of what?—of many wretched buildings and some dirty alleys. For I deny that any one elegant street or building in this city is more obstructed by trees than is necessary to the comfort of the inhabitants, and to give beauty to the prospect. Men of taste have always thought that a due mixture of trees and buildings; the beauties of nature and art united. Elegant architecture discovered through luxuriant foliage, compose an exhibition truly beautiful and sublime—but it seems your honors think otherwise; this clause therefore should run thus—"Whereas a moderate proportion of trees are a great ornament and decoration to a city; and whereas we have no taste whatever for elegance and ornament, *Be it therefore enacted,"* &c.—As to these trees obstructing the passage, this I must absolutely deny. They have modestly posted themselves as close to the gutters as they can stand, leaving both footway and cartway free and open. If, however, any straggler should be found so obstructing the passage, let him be put to death; I have nothing to say in his behalf.—But it is alledged that they, the aforesaid trees, disturb and disorder the water-courses and foot-ways by the extension of their roots. If so, cut off the offending root; but do not destroy the whole tree. When justice exceeds her limits, she forfeits her name. This evil is a very modern discovery; and if instances should be demanded to support the charge, they must be carefully looked for; I aver that the fact is not generally true. Lastly, trees communicate fire. A tree hath no greater enemy in nature than fire—cut him into inch pieces—grind him into sawdust, it will still exist as wood for many, many years. Fire alone can suddenly dissipate its component parts, and destroy its name. Whilst it hath life, it obstinately resists this consuming foe—nor can any art make a green tree burn—no, nor a green log neither—as many a cursing cook can tell.

But besides the charges laid in the bill, two others have been suggested against these poor trees, viz. That they obstruct the operation of the engines in case of fire; and that they are not well affected to the present government, because they remained in the city when the enemy took possession of it. As to the first, little can be said; when the case occurs let the offender be removed, which may be speedily done; but to depopulate a whole city for the possible offence of a few individuals, is certainly neither law nor reason.—As to the second, it will not, I apprehend, be contended at this day, that the leaving the city or not on the approach of the enemy is the true line of distinction between *Whig* and *Tory*. It must be confessed *we* remained when others fled. We *stood our ground,* and we suffered in our country's cause. Turn, worthy Senators, turn your eyes to yonder fields—look towards the banks of Schuylkill. Where are now those verdant groves that used to grace the prospect? Where are those venerable oaks, that o'er the evening walk of sober citizen, of musing bard, of sportive youths or amorous nymphs and swains, were wont to spread their all inviting gloom?—Alas, nought now remain but lifeless stumps, that moulder in the summer's heat and winter's frost; the habitations fit of poisonous fungi, toads and ever gnawing worms.—*Hinc illae Lachrymae!*—These were thy feats, *O Howe!*[7]—Excuse, great Sirs, this *weakness* of a *post*—or rather join your sympathising tears with mine. The loss is yours—a loss, the importance of which you have not, perhaps, duly considered, and which I shall now endeavour to bring into view.

Having shewn the rank my fellow trees hold in the scale of *beings*, their capacities of pleasure and pain; having also obviated the charges brought against them, and touched upon their sufferings in the great political revolution of this country; I come now to the last argument I intended for their defence. I mean the great use and importance they are of to mankind. And here I shall be very concise, avoiding all those circumstances in which trees obviously contribute to the pleasure, use and profit of men, as these must be well known to your honors, and confining myself to one very serious consideration.—I mean, how far the healths and lives of the inhabitants of this city are concerned in the business you are upon. A few hours are sufficient to execute this fatal law; but it will take years to repair the damage when you shall have discovered your error. Consider, therefore, Oh rash and capricious mortals! what you are about to do, whilst consideration may be of use. Caution is never too late, repentance may be. Know that these trees, whom you are about to extirpate, are your best, your safest Physicians. The health of your citizens depends upon their growth, and you are now to decide, not only upon the existence of a few trees, but the lives of hundreds of your fellow citizens. I say, these trees are your best, your safest Physicians. They have published no books, therefore they have no systems to defend; their practice is ever uniform, dictated by nature and established by success, and therefore they make no

7. During the occupation of Philadelphia, General Howe had been forced to cut down groves of trees within the city for firewood (Scharf and Westcott, *History of Philadelphia,* 1:365).

whimsical experiments on their patients—experiments, uncertain in every thing but destruction and death—In a word, they have no occasion to kill *one hundred* in order to know how to cure *one.* In the autumn they modestly drop their foliage, to admit the comfortable rays of the sun to your dwellings, their leaves being then of no further use to you; but no sooner does the spring advance, but they arm themselves in your defence—they see the enemy approach—innumerable little deaths in various subtle forms. These are, by the fermenting heats of Summer, generated in every pool, gutter and common-sewer, and in all the murkey filth of your city. No sooner have the poisonous atoms acquired sufficient malignity, but they leave their native beds and float in air. One of these, inhaled, infects the blood, and soon a husband, son or father falls. To prevent this, the friendly tree spreads its broad and numerous foliage—every leaf is extended to intercept and absorb the floating mischief; and thus receiving and digesting the noxious particles (harmless to them) they purify the ambient air. This important philosophy was discovered by *Priestly,* improved by *Ingen-housz,* and will be prosecuted by *Fontana* to the great enlargement of human knowledge.[8]—The enemy had studied *Priestly* when they cut the trees from yonder plains, hoping to leave the atmosphere poisoned for your destruction. Is it not obvious that diseases most prevail when vegetation ceases? About the middle of August, most leaves have acquired their utmost growth; they are saturated with the noxious effluvia; they can no longer perform their friendly office; and

8. The post has been reading Jan Ingen Housz, *Experiment upon Vegetables, discovering their great Power of Purifying the Common Air in the Sun-shine, and of Inspiring it in the Shade and at Night. To which is joined, a new Method of examining the accurate Degree of Salubrity of the Atmosphere* (London, 1779). Ingen Housz acknowledges his great debt to Joseph Priestley, who first found that plants gave off beneficial gas, but the post's allusion is to a statement that Priestley had developed a device ("eudiometer") for testing the quality of air, and that the Abbé Felice Fontana, Italian naturalist, was then (1779) improving that device (Howard S. Reed, ed., *Chronica Botanica,* 2 [1949], 320).

therefore from that time to the first frost of the season (which effectually concludes the generation of these pernicious airs) sickness and deaths are most frequent. This use of the vegetable tribe seems to be a modern discovery, unless we may suppose it to have been known to the Indians of America; because a leaf pasted on the breast is, amongst them, the insignium of a Physician.

And will you then, Oh guardians of the people! will you by a fatal decree banish from amongst you those salutary citizens, to whom you are so much indebted for the blessing of health, without which every other blessing must remain un-enjoyed? And what advantage do you propose to yourselves by such a measure? Your streets and alleys, indeed, will not be obstructed by trees, but they will be obstructed by lengthened funerals and mournful processions—I shall not prolong the subject—If your honors will but ballance the imaginary good, with the real dangers that must attend such a measure, I am confident that your zeal for the public safety will induce you to remove, not the trees from this city, but the 12th section from the bill before the House.

I have but one thing more to add, and that is, that by the 15th section of your constitution, you are enjoined not to pass any law, except on occasions of sudden necessity, until the next session after the same hath been proposed and published for consideration. No such necessity appears in the present case. The roots and branches of these devoted trees will not increase to such a ruinous and enormous size between this and the next sessions of Assembly, as to render immediate amputation necessary. I would be far from supposing this House capable of malice or partiality; but must observe that this bill hath been hurried through the forms of legislation with unusual speed. You have spent much precious time in considering whether A or B should sit for a certain time in a certain chair; but do not hesitate to doom to death a number of quiet, harmless, and beneficent citizens, without remorse, without enquiry, without the common forms of law."

Here the Orator ceased and was dumb. The House was more surprized at the manner, than attentive to the matter of this speech. The question was put, and the clause passed without a dissenting voice, notwithstanding the importunate eloquence of this *philosophic post.*

SILVESTER.

*Pennsylvania Gazette 21 August 1782.*

# *INTELLIGENCE EXTRAORDINARY*

On Saturday, 21 June 1783, a mob of some 300 soldiers demonstrated outside the State House, petitioning Congress for long-overdue pay. They posted pickets at the doors, shouted and milled about, but otherwise behaved peacefully while awaiting a reply. If the sight of the milling troops was alarming, the rhetoric of their petition was even more so: After demanding authority to appoint their own arbiters, the soldiers went on, "You will immediately issue such authority, and deliver it to us, or otherwise we shall instantly let in those injured soldiers upon you, and abide by the consequence. You have only twenty minutes to deliberate upon this important matter" (*Pennsylvania Gazette*, 24 September 1783). Adjourned for the weekend, Congress hastily regrouped, appealing to Pennsylvania officials to call out the militia. Seeing no immediate threat from the troops, hesitating to antagonize them, and fearing that the militia would rather join than fight them, the state officials procrastinated during Sunday and Monday. On Tuesday, out of pique or terror, Congress passed a resolution abhorring the insult to the nation, then adjourned to rural Princeton.

Philadelphians, at first alarmed by the mutiny, later relieved at the troops' peaceful demeanor, then amused at Congressional panic over a threat more illusory than real, now realized that Congress meant to decamp for good. On Wednesday, President John Dickinson of the Executive Council invoked the powers of the state to subpoena the leaders—"A Capt. *Carberry*, deranged, and a Lieut. *Sullivan*"—only to find they had fled for their lives. Dickinson called the remaining troops to the State House, lectured them on their bad manners, then told them to go back to their barracks. They obeyed instantly. Thereupon the people of Philadelphia petitioned Congress to return.

From rural New Jersey, Congress replied on 30 June, assuring Philadelphians that there was no intention of slighting their patriotism or police power, but that orderly legislative business could not flourish where threats of force or violence went unchecked, and therefore Princeton was preferable. But after a summer at Princeton, Elbridge Gerry introduced a proposal that Congress meet at two sites in alternate sessions for the mutual convenience of eastern and southern representatives. As adopted on 21 October, the plan called for alternate sessions of equal length at Trenton and Annapolis until new facilities could be erected at neighboring sites. It was this scheme that sparked Hopkinson's proposal for a swinging Congress.

The great Revolution in America will undoubtedly involve many circumstances of considerable importance and curious speculation;—none, perhaps, more remarkable than this—that the philosophical world may expect to be entertained with a phœnomenon in mechanics altogether new, and which cannot fail of engaging their closest attention. The Americans, having observed the unstable operations of European governments, and the irregularities to which every political system is liable, have invented a method of regulating the affairs of their empire by *actual Mechanism*. For this purpose, an immense *Pendulum* hath been constructed, of which the point of suspension is fixed somewhere in the orbit of the planet *Mars*, and the *Bob* is composed of certain heterogenous matter, of great specific gravity, called the *American Congress*. This Pendulum is to vibrate between Annapolis, on the Chesapeake, and Trenton, on the Delaware, a range of about 180 miles. It will require the most subtile mathematical investigations to ascertain the true line of motion of this *heavy Bob*. It is certain, however, that it will not move in a *streight line*, nor in a cycloid, nor in a parabola, nor in a hyperbola, or in any other known curve; but will have a motion *peculiar to itself*, forming *a crooked line*, the properties of which cannot be ascertained by the present system of mathematics.

Altho' the oscillations of this pendulum will not be performed in, yet they will average, equal times. Two vibrations must be performed in two years, yet those vibrations may bear no determinate proportion to each other. This will depend altogether upon the specific gravity of the bob, which, being very variable, will render the oscillations equally variable with respect to one another. And, what is very extraordinary, although, in all other instances, the more ponderous a body is the more it is disposed to rest, and the shorter and slower will its vibrations be, it will be the reverse in this case, since the bob will be inclined to motion, in direct proportion as the matter of which it is composed shall be more or less dull and heavy.

By the oscillations of this pendulum and its heavy bob are the thirteen wheels of the American machine to be regulated; and it is expected that the different combinations of motions, the actings and counter-actings, the checks and counter-checks, of the moving parts will so balance each other, as to produce, in the final result, a movement so perfectly equable, that the great desiderata, viz. the perpetual motion, and the discovery of longitude, will no longer puzzle the brains and drain the purses of the seekers in science.

But the most entertaining consequence of this improvement in politics will be, the rendering visible the locomotive faculties of the several powers of Europe; so far, at least, as the same may be ascertained by their Envoys and Ambassadors. For, as they must all follow the movements of the American bob, they will do this according to the natural genius of the countries to which they respectively belong. The volatile and active will always keep within reach of the object of pursuit, the careless and indolent will loiter by the way, and the dull and phlegmatic be so distanced, that, by the time they shall have arrived at one of the limits of the oscillation, they will find it necessary to tack about, and pursue the pendulum in its return to the other. In order to render this alternate peregrination as convenient as may be to their Ministers, the several powers of Europe are to raise by contribution the sum of four hundred thousand guineas, for the purpose of levelling the roads between Annapolis and Trenton, removing obstructions, building bridges, and erecting houses of residence in each of those towns, if those can properly be called houses of residence where the inhabitants are to have no rest.

Some have thought, that when this *monstrous* pendulum shall be once set in motion, it will not be confined to the proposed limits, but will, by its great weight (contrary to the usual laws of gravity) enlarge its field of action, and acquire a velocity, which will cause it to swing from New-Hampshire to Georgia.

A further improvement hath also been suggested, which is this—Many philosophers have been of the opinion that the most regular and proper motion of a pendulum would be, to cause it to swing in a circle (and not in a vertical plane, as the common practice is) so that the string or rod may describe a perfect cone, of which the apex will be in the point of suspension, and the base formed by the circumference of the horizontal plane in which the bob moves. Should this idea prove just (which Mr. Rittenhouse[1] has been directed to ascertain) the revolutions of America will be performed in a circle, whose diameter, north and south, will be from a point in St. John's river to the mouth of the Missisippi, and west and east, from the Lake in the Woods to an unknown distance in the Atlantic ocean.[2] The only inconvenience will be, the cutting a circular road for the accommodation of foreign Ministers and the officers of Congress, and providing sufficient ships at the point, where the said line of circumvolution shall leave the continent to enter upon the waters of the Atlantic, in order that their Excellencies and their Honours may be attendant on this new sublunary planet in every part of its orbit.

A. B.

*Pennsylvania Gazette 29 October 1783.*

---

1. Foremost mathematician and astronomer in the American Philosophical Society, David Rittenhouse (1732–96) first gained renown at the age of twenty-nine when he constructed an orrery.
2. By the Treaty of Paris, negotiated in the fall of 1782 but not ratified until 3 September 1783, boundaries of the United States were set on a line running from the mouth of the St. Croix River northward to the St. John River, westward to the Lake of the Woods, then south along the Mississippi to the 31st parallel, and east along the southern boundary of Georgia.

# *SUMMARY OF LATE PROCEEDINGS*

A month after reporting the "Intelligence Extraordinary," Hopkinson published a sequel in an extraordinary medium, the *Freeman's Journal.* Since the time a year-and-a-half earlier when its writers had roasted him unmercifully, the *Journal* had suffered a transformation. It had itself been embroiled in a controversy with a new paper, the *Independent Gazetteer,* edited by Eleazar Oswald—a quarrel Hopkinson celebrated in the long fable about Philadelphia politics he did not publish, "A Full and True Account of a Terrible Uproar," in which Kitty Oswald and Fanny Belly, two nursemaids, come close to pulling hair. In their real-life quarrel Oswald invited Bailey to duel, a threat that served to temper the subsequent tone of the *Freeman's Journal.*

The satire Hopkinson now published in its columns posed a noncontroversial question about the compatibility of two measures recently passed by Congress. On 7 August, after four months of deliberation, Congress had resolved to erect a bronze equestrian statue honoring General Washington, to be created by the finest available sculptor in Europe from designs executed by a Congressional committee. The concern now raised was the provision that the statue be erected "at the place where the residence of Congress shall be established" (*Freeman's Journal,* 3 September 1783). Apparently no one other than Hopkinson noticed that this resolution required alignment with the resolution passed in October establishing dual residences—an oversight he now set out to correct.

A summary of some late proceedings
in a certain great assembly.

A Member, in the course of debate, took occasion to mention the resolve respecting the alternate residence of the house in two fœderal towns, at two hundred miles distance from each other; and although he acknowledged himself out of order, as the resolve had already been debated and past, yet he begged leave to draw their attention to a circumstance which perhaps had escaped notice at the time the resolution was adopted—which was this—That some months before, the house had solemnly resolved that a certain *equestrian statue* should be erected in the place where that house should fix its *permanent residence,* and he requested to know in what manner the house proposed to execute this resolve, under the present system of a *peregrinating* instead of a *permanent* residence.

This observation struck the house with great force, and many looked upon it as an invincible difficulty, and that the two resolves were altogether irreconcilable with each other. But the ingenious member who had planned the scheme of the two fœderal towns,[1] soon relieved them from their embarrassment, by declaring—That he had been well aware of this objection, and looked for it at the time the resolve in question was under debate; when, indeed, he should not have been so ready to answer it as at present. But that he was now prepared to obviate the difficulty that had been started; and should in a day or two bring in his scheme at large, as he only waited for certain drawings to be complcated, which were already in great forwardness.

The attention of the house being strongly drawn to the subject of this promise, they earnestly requested him to give them, *instanter,* some idea of his design.

The ingenious member, thus urged, said, that he was sensible his device must greatly suffer by being exhibited in a partial, imperfect manner; nevertheless, he could not refuse to gratify the impatience of the house, trusting to their candour, that they would not form a hasty judgment of his scheme, but wait till they should see the drawings exhibited, which he was preparing, and an explanation of the whole more at large. His design, he said, was this—not only to comply with the spirit of the resolve respecting the *equestrian statue,* but to make that very resolve conducive to the scheme of the two fœderal towns. The spirit and intention of the resolve respecting the *equestrian statue,* he observed, was no more than this, that the said statue should always be where the house should sit. To effect which, nothing more was necessary than to adjourn the statue whenever and

1. Immortalized in the term "gerrymander," Elbridge Gerry (1744–1814), veteran representative from Massachusetts, was humorless. Hopkinson here parodies his prolix debating style.

wherever they should adjourn the house; which might easily be done by mounting it upon wheels—But this was not all—for if *the horse* should be constructed of large size, and framed with timbers like thc hull of a ship, it would become a most convenient and proper vehicle to transport the members themselves, with their books, papers, &c. from one fœderal town to the other.—

And added that the drawings he had mentioned, were designed to exhibit such a construction of the body of a horse as might most conveniently answer this purpose; wherein would be shewn the seats intended for the respective members, the places of the president and secretary, and a little closet in the *intestinum rectum* for the secret papers of the house; provision also being made for light and air, and every other convenience necessary in so great a design.

He confessed he had taken his idea from the *Grecian horse* used at the siege of Troy, and been searching Homer and all his translators, commentators and annotators, in hopes of finding some description of the internal construction of that famous horse, but receiving no help from these sources, he had been obliged to depend upon his own ingenuity and the advice of an able ship builder, whom he had consulted, and who was now making the drawings he proposed to lay before the house.

This device of the ingenious member was much applauded—but a still more ingenious member rose up, and said,—That the gentleman who spoke last, had, in some measure anticipated a project he had been preparing to offer. But as the design he had formed was upon a much larger scale than that which had been just now suggested, he should not withhold it from the house, although he confest it was planned on much the same principles. The difficulty respecting the statue, he said, had not indeed occured to him; but one, of at least equal importance, had—which was the enormous expence of building *two* fœderal towns, when *one* might be sufficient for all purposes. To obviate this, he would propose, that there should be two places of *alternate permanent residence,* agreeable to the late resolve, and but one fœderal town; which town should be built upon a large platform, mounted on a great number of wheels, and be drawn by a great number of horses.

This, he observed, would be attended with many and great conveniencies—It would render the immense expence of building two fœderal towns unnecessary—It would avoid the trouble and confusion of packing and unpacking, arranging and deranging, their books and papers at every adjournment—and it would save much precious time, in as much as there need be no interruption whatever of their proceedings, since the business of the house might be *going on* whilst the house itself was *going on;* and *motions* be not only made in the house, but the house itself *make motions;* so that, what with the motions of the members, the motions of the house, and the motions of the whole fœderal town, all the powers of government would be in constant action for the good of the empire.

He then proceeded to shew that such a scheme was neither absurd in itself nor impracticable. It was not absurd, he said, because nature, who does nothing improper, had given instances; for example, in the snail, the tortoise, and many other animals—Neither was it impracticable, as he undertook plainly to evince. He asserted that he had himself seen in England a certain tinker who had mounted a small house on wheels, which contained a bed and all the utensils of his trade; that it was drawn about by a single horse; so that when he had exhausted all the custom of one village he removed, *cum omnibus appurtenantibus,* to another; and by that means found a constant circulation of employ. —But I have an instance said he directly in point; I mean that of the empress of Russia, who, when she moves her court from Petersburgh to Moscow, is accommodated with elegant apartments, built on sleds, and drawn by fifty horses, over a tract of snow many hundred miles in extent.—But it may be objected continued this ingenious member, that these are only instances of a single room, or of two or three apartments being rendered moveable by machinery; but the idea of a whole town, a federal town, an imperial town, becoming thus transitory, is altogether impracticable, unless by art of magic.—But I am not altogether unprepared to answer this objection. It is a great mark of weakness to suppose every thing impossible which we cannot conceive. Fools always wonder improperly. They see a jack weight descend without surprize, but exclaim with amazement at the movements of an orrery; whereas, in fact, there is infinitely more mystery in the descent of a jack weight than in the most complicated movements of an orrery. I shall not now undertake to describe minutely the manner in which our federal town may be rendered *itinerant* —this I reserve for a future day—but to shew that the thing is at least not impossible, I beg leave to read a passage from a book I have in my hand. It is entituled, A Voyage to the Moon by Cyrano Bergerac—Page 112 and 104.

—"At this our young host enquired from his father, what was the hour? who replying it had already struck eight, he very angrily asked him, How he dared neglect calling him at seven, as he had ordered? When he knew very well the houses were to begin their journey the next day, the walls of the town being already gone. The good man told him, that since his setting down to table, a proclamation had been made, forbidding the houses to set out before the day after to-morrow.

—"In order to turn the discourse, I intreated him to inform me, what was meant by the removal of the town, and if the houses and walls really travelled! Dear stranger, said he, our buildings are of two sorts, the *moveable* and the *sedentary.* The *moveable,* in one of which you are now, I am about to describe. They are composed, as you see, of a very light wood; and at the building of them, the architect places four strong wheels under the foundation of the walls. Six large pair of bellows are placed with their noses horizontally to the wings of the upper story; so that when a town is to be removed (which is always done as the seasons change) several large sails are unfolded before the nose of these bellows, which, being set at work, discharge the wind so very strongly upon them that the houses are set in motion; and by the violence of the gust, which drives them forward, they are enabled to travel upwards of an hundred leagues in eight days."—

The very ingenious member quoted his authority with no small marks of triumph, and observed in closing the book, that what had been done, might be done again—that he should however improve upon the plan of his *lunatic* brethren, by causing his town to move bodily with all its contents, rights, privileges and appurtenances; and not by single houses, which he apprehended would be apt to occasion much confusion on the road. He concluded with saying that the only thing he should ask of the house would be to proclaim a two days *fast* previous to every adjournment; not only with a view of rendering the burthen of so great a machine as light as possible, but also to avoid too great a perplexity of *motions,* during the journey.

The house was astonished at the extensive genius of the projecting member, and immediately adjourned; having first recommended it to each other to consider, against the next meeting, what objections could possibly be made to the last proposed scheme.

A. B.

*The Freeman's Journal 26 November 1783.*

# *COMMON AMUSEMENTS*

The *Pennsylvania Packet* of 1 March 1785 carried Hopkinson's bagatelle celebrating two local controversies then eddying through the columns of the Philadelphia press. The more serious of the two featured an exchange of insults between Provost John Ewing of the University of Pennsylvania and the terrible-tempered Dr. Benjamin Rush who had been promoting with accustomed vigor a newly established Presbyterian college at Carlisle. Rush was convinced that the university was a godless institution, that a new college was necessary to restore religion to science, and that youth of the western part of the state deserved a school of their own. His *Hints for Establishing a College at Carlisle* (1782) convinced powerful Presbyterians centered in that locality "to entrench themselves in schools of learning . . . the nurseries of power and influence," and they had exerted sufficient pressure in the assembly to overcome university opposition by four votes. Dickinson College—named for the President of the State, John Dickinson—was duly chartered in September 1783.

The fight for the charter left wounds slow to heal. "From that time," confessed Rush in the *Packet* for 17 February 1785, "the Revd. Dr. Ewing has been my steady and implacable enemy." Rush accused him now of trying to dissuade an eminent Scottish educator from accepting leadership of the college. Ewing denied it, accusing Rush of trying to subvert higher education by raising religious issues, calling the university anti-Episcopalian in Philadelphia, anti-Presbyterian in Carlisle, when, in fact, both the trustees and faculty represented many shades of denominational Protestantism. Thus their controversy swirled.

The minor controversy featured cross-accusations by musician William Brown and John Bentley, who produced a series of "City Concerts of Vocal and Instrumental Music." Brown accused Bentley of bad conduct in not attending a benefit concert by Brown and by dissuading two members of the orchestra from attending also. Bentley countered that Brown had refused his offer to lend him a harpsichord. Brown replied that the harpsichord was too small. Their recriminations in the press tickled Hopkinson to echo the rhyme John Byrom composed earlier in the century to memorialize the rivalry between Handel and Bononcini—

> Strange all this Difference should be
> 'Twixt Tweedle-dum and Tweedle-dee.

A man who is disposed to be entertained may extract amusement from the most common occurrences of life. Objects strike the eye and incidents affect the mind very differently in different persons. Some men accustom themselves to see every thing in a ludicrous point of view, others in a serious light, and the multitude are content with mere perception; that is, barely seeing and hearing, without making any further use of their senses. These variations of temper are founded in the original constitution of the party—the humourist was funny and roguish when a boy; following the invincible propensity of his nature, he acquires by habit, an amazing facility in associating ludicrous ideas to the most ordinary and seemingly the most barren incidents of life.

His eye immediately discovers any singularity of countenance or manner, because he is always hunting after singularities; and something diverts him in the most common transactions, because he is always looking for diversion.

I have, myself, some tincture of this disposition, and when disengaged from more serious business, I sally forth with a view of *being entertained.* It requires no great effort of imagination to suppose most of the people in this great city actually *mad.* Impress'd with this idea, I observe the countenance, gait and manner of every one I meet, and amuse myself by classing him under some species of frenzy or other.—One fellow drives along with such heedless impetuosity that he treads in the gutters instead of stepping over them, and runs against the posts which he might easily avoid—I do not hesitate to mark him down in my list of *lunatics*—Another has such strong marks of anxiety express'd in his visage, that his whole soul seems absorbed in some sale or purchase; I mark him down *avariciously mad.* A third is haranguing at a corner with great earnestness to two or three ignoramus's, who swallow his detail with open ears and open mouths; I mark the orator *politically mad,* and his hearers *foolishly mad.* I see a fourth in a violent passion cursing and swearing like a sailor in a storm, him I score *raving mad*—but there is no end to the variety of characters that present, and of course no end to the entertainment.

At another time, I apply to the streets for a different species of diversion. I walk round a square and attend to all the scraps and fragments of conversation which I can pick up *en passant.* As soon as I get home I write down these on separate pieces of paper; and then amuse myself with arranging them in such order, as to produce, if possible, some apparent connection and sense. If this can't be done, I make another excursion and collect more materials; till out of a great number I am enabled to accomplish my purpose.—For example—

What's the price of butter to-day?
It will bring 4 s. a gallon by the hogshead.—

Is your cousin married?
She will be launch'd next week.

He will carry you thro' thick and thin and never tire—
Ah! be sure, we must support the constitution.

She's a d—d fine girl—faith!—
But she sprung a leak and was obliged to be hove down.

The funding bill will never pass—
No, friend, the insurers must bear the loss, we have nothing to do with it.

They say *Longchamps* will be given up[1]—
That's my man—no it's mine—I swear it's mine, it rolled into the gutter—you lie! it was mine rolled into the gutter—it struck against that gentleman's foot, and he kick'd it into the gutter—didn't it Tom—didn't it Jack—You lie, I say it didn't—did it Cuff?—did it Pompey?—Here a boxing match.—

But my present fancy is to suppose the public news papers as so many real theatres, on which some play or farce is daily exhibited for my amusement—About nine in the morning my servant brings in the paper—very well—I eat my breakfast whilst I suppose a chapter from Cook's Voyage is reading by way of prologue.[2] My daughter is practising her lesson on the harpsichord; this serves for the music of the orchestra—When I have breakfasted I desire her to leave off, lest her playing should interrupt my reading—the curtain then rises and the play begins.—For instance

---

1. During the previous year Pennsylvania had been engaged in a jurisdictional dispute with France over punishing Charles Longchamps for assault and battery on the French consul-general in Philadelphia. France insisted that he be extradited, but the state supreme court ruled that he should not be given up.
2. The *Packet* had been serializing *A Voyage to the Pacific Ocean* (1784).

SCENE PHILADELPHIA.
Enter a Doctor of *Divinity* and a Doctor of *Physic.*

A familiar dialogue immediately ensues, in which each performer endeavours to display the character of his antagonist in as striking a manner as possible, to my great entertainment—I then imagine I see a professional battle—The divine throws texts of scripture in the teeth of his adversary, and endeavours to hamper him with the cords of logical conclusions, whilst the physician squirts clysters in the face of the divine, and claps cantharides on his back. But the most comical and diverting part of the scene is, to see one of the learned professors *hoist* the university; he exposes it's naked skin, and exclaims with admiration—'Oh charming! behold and see, what a *broad bottom* is here'[3]—whereupon the other learned professor immediately *hoists* Dickinson college, and with equal eloquence extolls it's *narrow bottom*—'Look, says the divine, at this capacious disk—on one side sits the *Pope,* on the other side sits *Luther;* and see how snug Calvin lies between them both'—'It's all wrong, replies the physician, *Calvin* has no business there—he will be chock'd—he will be suffocated—he will be squeez'd to death—here is a *narrow bottom,* more fit for his accommodation—he is a usurper *there,* but *this* is his own flesh and blood.' From words they soon proceed to blows, the divine is heated with zeal, he vociferates—'The sword of the Lord and of Gideon'—and forthwith flogs away at the *narrow bottom* of poor *Carlisle.* The physician is also enraged—'By the dust of Hypocrates and the bones of Boerhave, says he, I'll be even with you'—and without further prelude, falls to scourging the *Pope, Luther,* and *Calvin* all at once, upon the *broad bum* of the university—But the scene changes—

---

3. This echoes Ewing's letter in the *Packet* for 9 February, insisting that the old trustees had been removed because, with respect to ecumenical representation, they had "narrowed the broad and catholic bottom of the institution."

Enter two *Musicians.*
(another battle.)

*Mr. Tweedle-dum* begins the attack with a full discord in a sharp third, and leaves it unresolved, which to be sure, is very shocking. *Mr. Tweedle-dee* replies in the natural key, but with a sharp third also, *Tweedle-dum* then changes the modulation and runs a rapid division, finishing with a chromatic *arpeggio* in a flat third; this is amazingly provoking, the parties are enraged, *Tweedle-dum* seizes the diapason-pipe of an organ, *Tweedle-dee* defends himself only with a silver mounted flute; and to it they go, blasting away at each other with astonishing vigour and dexterity: methinks I hear the shrill tones of the flute now ranging through the upper octave, and maintaining acknowledged superiority, and now again descending into the flowery plains of the fruitful tenor and yielding to the powerful vibrations of the dreadful organ-pipe.

Thus it is, that by the help of imagination, and a talent for viewing circumstances in a singular point of view, I am enabled to find entertainment in occurrences which are scarcely noticed by others. But I never make sport of matters really serious; the miseries, misfortunes, and sufferings of our fellow creatures can never be proper subjects of ridicule; but the passions, follies, and excentricities of mankind are surely lawful occasions of laughter. —*Viva la bagatelle.*

A. B.

*Pennsylvania Packet 1 March 1785.*

# *WHITEWASHING*

As if illustrating the point of "Common Amusements"—"I am enabled to find entertainment in occurrences which are scarcely noticed by others."—Hopkinson's next humorous piece for the *Packet* was this delightful report on the national ritual of spring cleaning, then called "whitewashing" after the practice described in the essay of brightening the walls after a winter of smoke and soot from open fires.

Gentlemen,

If you think the enclosed copy of a letter from a gentleman in America to his friend in Europe, will afford your readers any entertainment, you are at liberty to insert it in your useful paper. A. B.

Dear Sir,

The peculiar customs of every country appear to strangers singular and absurd; but the inhabitants consider those very customs as highly proper and even indispensibly necessary. Long habit imposes upon the understanding any thing that is not in itself immediately destructive or pernicious. The religion of a country is scarcely held in greater sanctity than its established customs; and it is almost as fruitless to attempt alterations in the one as in the other. Any interference of government to reform national customs, however trivial and absurd, never fails to produce the greatest discontents, and sometimes dangerous convulsions; of this there are frequent instances in history. Bad customs can only be removed by the same means that established them, viz. by imperceptible gradations and the constant example and influence of the higher class of the people. We are apt to conclude that the fashions and customs of our own country are the most rational and proper, because the eye and the understanding have long since been reconciled to them; but when we see or read of foreign manners, we either ridicule or condemn them; and yet the foreigner will defend his national habits with full as much plausibility, as we can our own. The truth is, that reason has very little to do in the matter, and nature less. All customs are arbitrary, and one nation hath as undoubted a right to fix its peculiarities as another. It is in vain to talk of convenience as a standard; for every thing becomes convenient by practice and habit.

I have read somewhere of a nation, in Africa (I think) which is governed by twelve counsellors.—When these counsellors are to meet on public business, twelve large earthen jars are set in two rows and filled with water; the counsellors, one after another, enter the apartment stark naked, and each leaps into a jar, where he sets up to the chin in water; when the jars are all filled with counsellors, they proceed to deliberate on the great concerns of the people.—This, to be sure, forms a very grotesque idea; but the object is to transact the public business. They have been accustomed to do it in this way, and can do it in no other. To them, therefore, it is rational and convenient. Indeed if we consider it impartially, there seems to be no reason why a counsellor may not be as wise in an earthen jar as in an elbow chair; or why the good of the people may not be as maturely considered, and as effectually promoted in the one as in the other.

The established manners of every country are the standards of propriety with the people who have adopted them, and every nation assumes the right of considering all deviations from their fashions and customs as barbarisms and absurdities. The Chinese have retained their laws and customs unaltered for ages immemorial; and although they have long had a free intercourse with European nations, and are well acquainted with their improvements in arts and modes of civilization, yet they are so far from being convinced of any superiority in the European manners, that their government takes the most serious precautions to prevent the barbarisms of other nations from taking root amongst them. It employs their utmost vigilance and attention to enjoy the benefits of commerce and at the same time guard against any innovations in the characteristic manners of their people.

Since the discovery of the Sandwich Islands in the South Sea, they have been visited by ships from different nations; but the inhabitants have shewn no inclination to prefer the dress and manners of foreigners to their own. It is even probable that they pity the ignorance of the Europeans they have seen, and hug themselves in the propriety of their own customs, and the superior advancement of their own civilization.

There is nothing new in these observations; and I had no intention of making them when I sat down, but they obtruded themselves upon me. My wish is to give you some account of the people of these new states; but I am far from being qualified for the purpose, having, as yet, seen little more than the cities of New-York and Philadelphia; I have discovered but few national singularities amongst them. Their customs and manners are nearly the same with those of England, which they have long been used to copy. For previous to the revolution, the Americans were, from their infancy, taught to look up to the English as patterns of perfection in all things. I have observed, however, one custom, which, for ought I know, is peculiar to this country. An account of it will serve to fill up the remainder of this sheet, and may afford you some amusement.

When a young couple are about to enter on the matrimonial state, a never-failing article in the marriage treaty is, that the lady shall have and enjoy the free and unmolested exercise of the rights of *white-washing*, with all its ceremonials, privileges and appurtenances. A young woman would forego the most advantageous connection, and even disappoint the warmest wish of her heart, rather than resign this invaluable right. You will wonder what this privilege of *white-washing* is:—I will endeavour to give you some idea of the ceremony, as I have seen it performed.

There is no season of the year in which the lady may not claim her privilege, if she pleases; but the latter end of May is most generally fixed upon for the purpose. The attentive husband may judge by certain prognostics when the storm is nigh at hand. If the lady grows unusually fretful, finds fault with the servants, is discontented with the children, and complains much of the nastiness of every thing about her, these are signs which ought not be neglected—yet they are not decisive; as they sometimes occur and go off again, without producing any further effect. But if, when the husband rises in the morning, he should observe in the yard a wheel-barrow with a quantity of lime in it, or should see certain buckets with lime dissolved in water, there is then no time to be lost—he immediately locks up the apartment or closet where his papers or his private property are kept, and putting the key in his pocket, betakes himself to flight.—For a husband, however beloved, becomes a perfect nuisance during this season of female rage; his authority is superceded, his commission is suspended, and the very scullion who cleans the brasses in the kitchen, becomes of more consideration and importance than him.—He has nothing for it, but to abdicate, and run from an evil which he can neither prevent or mollify.

The husband gone, the ceremony begins, the walls are in a few minutes stripped of their furniture,—paintings, prints, and looking-glasses lie in huddled heaps about the floors, the curtains are torn from the testers, the beds crammed into the windows, chairs and tables, bedsteads and cradles crowd the yard, and the garden fence bends beneath the weight of carpets, blankets, cloth cloaks, old coats, and ragged breeches.—*Here* may be seen the lumber of the kitchen forming a dark and confused mass, for the fore-ground of the picture, grid-irons and frying-pans, rusty shovels and broken tongs, spits and pots, joint-stools and the fractured remains of rush-bottomed chairs. *There* a closet has disgorged its bowels, rivetted plates and dishes, halves of China bowls, cracked tumblers, broken wine glasses, phials of forgotten physic, papers of unknown powders, seeds and dried herbs, handfuls of old corks, tops of tea pots, and stoppers of departed decanters; from the rag-hole in the garret to the rat-hole in the cellar, no place escapes unrummaged. It would seem as if the day of general doom was come, and the utensils of the house were dragged forth to judgement. In this tempest the words of *Lear* naturally present, and might, with little alteration, be made strictly applicable.

> "————Let the great Gods,
> "That keep this dreadful pudder o'er our heads,
> "Find out their enemies now. Tremble thou wretch,
> "That hast within thee undivulged crimes
> "Unwhipt of justice!————"
> "————Close pent up guilt

"Rise your concealing continents, and ask
"These dreadful summoners grace!-"[1]

This ceremony compleated, and the house thoroughly evacuated, the next operation is to smear the walls and ceilings of every room and closet with brushes, dipped in a solution of lime, called *white-wash;* to pour buckets of water over every floor, and scratch all the partitions and wainscots with rough brushes wet with soap-suds, and dipped in stonecutter's sand. The windows by no means escape the general deluge. A servant scrambles out upon the penthouse, at the risk of her neck, and with a mug in her hand and a bucket within reach, she dashes away innumerable gallons of water against the glass panes; to the great annoyance of the passengers in the street.

I have been told that an action at law was once brought against one of these water nymphs, by a person who had a new suit of cloaths spoiled by this operation; but, after long argument, it was determined by the whole court, that the action would not lie, in as much as the defendant was in the exercise of a legal right, and not answerable for the consequences; and so the poor gentleman was doubly nonsuited; for he lost not only his suit of cloaths, but his suit at law.

These smearings and scratchings, washings and dashings, being duly performed, the next ceremonial is to cleanse and replace the distracted furniture; you may have seen a house-raising or a ship-launch, when all the hands within reach are collected together—recollect, if you can, the hurry-bustle-confusion-and noise of such a scene, and you will have some idea of this cleaning match—the misfortune is that the sole object is to make things clean: it matters not how many useful, ornamental, or valuable articles are mutulated or suffer death under the operation; a mahogany chair

1. *King Lear,* III.ii.49–53, 57–59. While "Rise" is a typographical error, "pudder" in l. 50 and "ask" in l. 58 show that Hopkinson used the Pope-Warburton edition (1747).

and carved frame undergo the same discipline; they are to be made clean at all events; but their preservation is not worthy of attention. For instance, a fine large engraving is laid flat upon the floor; smaller prints are piled upon it until the superincumbent weight cracks the glasses of the lower tier: but this is of no consequence.—A valuable picture is placed leaning against the sharp corner of a table; others are made to lean against that, until the pressure of the whole forces the corner of the table through the canvas of the first—The frame and glass of a fine print are to be cleaned, the spirit and oil used on this occasion are suffered to leak through and spoil the engraving, no matter, if the glass is clean and the frame shines, it is sufficient; the rest is not worthy of consideration. An able arithmetician hath made an accurate calculation, founded on long experience, and discovered that the losses and destruction incident to two white-washings are equal to one removal, and three removals equal to one fire.

The cleansing frolic over, matters begin to resume their pristine appearance—The storm abates, and all would be well again; but it is impossible that so great a convulsion in so small a community should not produce some further effects. For two or three weeks after the operation, the family are usually afflicted with sore eyes or sore throats, occasioned by the caustic quality of the lime; or with severe colds from the exhalations of wet floors and damp walls.

I know a gentleman here who is fond of accounting for every thing in a philosophical way. He considers this which I have called a custom, as a real periodical disease, peculiar to the climate. His train of reasoning is ingenious and whimsical: but I am not at leisure to give you the detail. The result was, that he found the distemper to be incurable; but after much study he conceived he had discovered a method to divert the evil he could not subdue. For this purpose he caused a small building, about twelve feet square, to be erected in his garden, and furnished with some ordinary chairs and tables; and a few prints of the cheapest sort were hung against the walls. His hope was, that when the white-washing frenzy seized the females of his family, they might repair to this apartment and scrub, and scour, and smear to their hearts content—and so spend the violence of the disease in this out-post, whilst he enjoyed himself in quiet at head-quarters. But the experiment did not answer his expectation—it was impossible it should, since a principal part of the gratification consists in the ladies having an uncontrouled right to torment her husband at least once in a year, and to turn him out of doors, and take the reigns of government into her own hands.

There is a much better contrivance than this of the philosopher's; which is to cover the walls of the house with paper—this is generally done; and tho' it cannot abolish, it at least shortens the period of female dominion. The paper is decorated with flowers of various fancies, and made so ornamental that the women have admitted the fashion without perceiving the design.

There is also another alleviation of the husband's distress—he generally has the privilege of a small room or closet for his books and papers, the key of which he is allowed to keep. This is considered as a priviledged place, and stands like the land of Goshen amidst the plagues of Egypt. But then he must be extremely cautious, and ever on his guard. For should he inadvertently go abroad and leave the key in his door, the house-maid, who is always on the watch for such an opportunity, immediately enters in triumph with buckets, brooms, and brushes, takes possession of the premises, and forthwith puts all his books and papers *to rights;* to his utter confusion, and sometimes serious detriment. For instance—

A gentleman was sued by the executors of a tradesman, on a charge found against him in the deceased's books, to the amount of £30. The defendant was strongly impressed with an idea that he had discharged the debt and taken a receipt; but as the transaction was of long standing, he knew not where to find the receipt. The suit went on in course, and the time approached when judgement would be obtained against him. He then sat seriously down to examine a large bundle of old papers, which he had untied and displayed on a table for the purpose. In the midst of his search, he was suddenly called away on business of importance—

he forgot to lock the door of his room. The house-maid, who had been long looking for such an opportunity, immediately entered with the usual implements, and with great alacrity fell to cleaning the room, and *putting things to rights*. The first object that struck her eye was the confused situation of the papers on the table; these were, without delay bundled together like so many dirty knives and forks; but in the action a small piece of paper fell unnoticed on the floor, which happened to be the very receipt in question: as it had no very respectable appearance, it was soon after swept out with the common dirt of the room, and carried in a dirt pan to the yard. The tradesman had neglected to enter the credit in his books; the defendant could find nothing to obviate the charge, and so judgement went against him for the debt and costs—A fortnight after the whole was settled, and the money paid, one of the children found the receipt amongst the dirt in the yard.

There is also another custom peculiar to the city of Philadelphia, and nearly allied to the former. I mean that of washing the pavements before the doors every Saturday evening. I at first took this to be a regulation of the police; but, on further enquiry, find it is a religious rite, preparatory to the Sabbath; and is, I believe, the only religious rite in which the numerous sectaries of this city perfectly agree. The ceremony begins about sunset and continues till ten or eleven at night. It is very difficult for a stranger to walk the streets on those evenings—he runs a continual risk of having a bucket of dirty water thrown against his legs; but a Philadelphian born is so much accustomed to the danger, that he avoids it with surprising dexterity. It is from this circumstance that a Philadelphian may be known any where by his gate. The streets of New-York are paved with rough stones, these indeed are not washed, but the dirt is so thoroughly swept from before the doors, that the stones stand up sharp and prominent, to the great inconvenience of those who are not accustomed to so rough a path. But habit reconciles every thing. It is diverting enough to see a Philadelphian at New-York—he walks the street with as much painful caution, as if his toes were covered with corns, or his feet lamed by the gout; whilst a New-Yorker, as little approving the plain masonry of Philadelphia, shuffles along the pavement like a parrot upon a mahogany table.

It must be acknowledged that the ablutions I have mentioned are attended with no small inconvenience; but the women would not be induced for any consideration to resign their privilege. Notwithstanding this, I can give you the strongest assurances that the women of America make the most faithful wives, and the most attentive mothers in the world; and I am sure you will join me in opinion, that if a married man is made miserable only for one week in a whole year, he will have no great cause to complain of the matrimonial bond.

This letter has run on to a length I did not expect; I therefore hasten to assure you that I am, as ever,

Yours &c. &c. &c.

*Pennsylvania Packet 18 June 1785.*

# *THE ART OF PAPER WAR*

In early August 1786, once again playing the role of the Swiftian "projector," Hopkinson satirized an inane public quarrel that had consumed a dozen full columns of the *Pennsylvania Packet* during the previous month. Antagonists were William Lewis, a long-winded, leading Quaker lawyer, and Hugh Moore, a disgruntled client who felt Lewis had not pursued a case of his with sufficient fervor. Lewis charged malevolent slander in an open letter two-and-a-half columns long and headed "To the Public" in a size of type more common to advertisements. The subsequent exchange of insults inflated to four-and-three-quarter columns by the end of the month, with the principals now joined by their respective seconds in a series of challenges to meet on the field of honor. The seconds continued their exchange but the principals fell silent after Hopkinson's satire appeared. His success was owing as much to his medium as to his wit. It was not uncommon for newspapers to show off the novelty or variety of new types, but Hopkinson—in extending the technique of his essay on portrait painting—now made the medium itself his message.

I mentioned in a former essay, that my greatest ambition is to become famous by the invention of some ingenious or useful project, which shall be generally approved and adopted. At the same time I communicated to the public a device which, from its novelty and convenience, I thought could not fail of success. In vain, however, have I looked for that applause which I still think justly due to the fruit of genius, ripened by the labours of the understanding. The author and his contrivance are no more thought of.

I have, at different periods, published many other devices of rare invention, which have all found the same fate. Whether the fault lies with me or the public, I will not presume to say: but as my love of fame is invincible, I shall go on projecting and contriving, in hopes some lucky hit may accomplish my purpose, and fulfil my desire. However, as I am now growing old in the business, experience and disappointments have taught me to be less sanguine in my expectations; and, like other authors, to depend more on a fortuitous possession of the public caprice, than on the intrinsic merits of my own performances.

My present design, which I offer with great modesty, respects an improvement in the art of printing—so as to make it expressive not only of an author's narrative, opinions or arguments, but also of the peculiarities of his temper, and the vivacity of his feelings.

As I have a great deal of literary honesty, I am ready to acknowledge, that I took the hint from an ingenious work of a *Mr. Steel* of London, who contrived and has published a scheme for noting down in certain musical characters the risings, fallings and various inflections of the human voice in common conversation, or public speaking.[1] So that not only the matter of an oration, but even the manner of the orator may be secured, and transmitted to posterity.

My contrivance has this advantage over his, that no new characters are necessary—those commonly used in printing are suffi-

1. Joshua Steele, *An Essay towards Establishing the Melody and Measure of Speech . . . by Certain Symbols* (1775; 2d ed. 1779).

cient for my purpose. Besides, his project is only calculated to ascertain the fortes, pianos, and various slides of the voice in speaking; whereas mine is intended to designate the fortes and pianos of the temper in writing.

My system is founded in a practice which Nature herself dictates, and which every one must have observed. I mean that of elevating the voice, in proportion to the agitation of the mind, or earnestness of the speaker—thus a reprimand is given in a higher tone than admonition, and a person in a fright or passion exerts his lungs according to the quantum of terror or rage with which he is affected. Now, I would have the degree of vociferation, such as *pianissimo, piano, forte, fortissimo,* with all the intermediate gradations, designated by the size of the letters which compose the emphatic words; and for this, the various species of types from

Pearl

up to

# Five line Pica

will afford an ample scale.

The ingenious authors of advertisements have, I confess, in some degree anticipated my device. We often see Stop Thief! Stop Thief! bawled out in

## Double Pica Italics.

The name of a ship to be sold, or some choice article to be disposed of, in of fuccefs. In vain, however, have I looked for that applaufe which I ftill think juftly due to the fruit of genius, ripened by the labours of the underftanding. The author and his contrivance are no more thought of.

I have, at different periods, publifhed many o- ther devices of rare invention, which have all found the fame fate. Whether the fault lies with me or the public, I will not prefume to fay: but as my love of fame is invincible, I fhall go on projecting and contriving, in hopes fome lucky hit may accomplifh my purpofe, and fulfil my defire. However, as I am now growing old in the bufinefs, experience and dif- appointments have taught me to be lefs fanguine in my expectations; and, like other authors, to depend more on a fortuitous poffeffion of the public caprice, than on the intrinfic merits of my own performances.

My prefent defign, which I offer with great mo- defty, refpects an improvement in the art of print- ing—fo as to make it expreffive not only of an au- thor's narrative, opinions or arguments, but alfo of the peculiarities of his temper, and the vivacity of his feelings.

As I have a great deal of literary honefty, I am ready to acknowledge, that I took the hint from an ingenious work of a Mr. Steel of London, who con trived and has publifhed a fcheme for noting down in certain mufical characters the rifings, fallings and various inflections of the human voice in common converfation, or public fpeaking. So that not only the matter of an oration, but even the manner of the orator may be fecured, and tranfmitted to pofterity.

My contrivance has this advantage over his, that no new characters are neceffary—thofe commonly ufed in printing are fufficient for my purpofe. Be- fides, his project is only calculated to afcertain the fortes, pianos, and various flides of the voice in fpeak- ing; whereas mine is intended to defignate the fortes and pianos of the temper in writing.

My fyftem is founded in a practice which Nature herfelf dictates, and which every one muft have ob- ferved. I mean that of elevating the voice, in pro- portion to the agitation of the mind, or earneftnefs of the fpeaker—thus a reprimand is given in a high- er tone than admonition, and a perfon in a fright or paffion exerts his lungs according to the quantum of terror or rage with which he is affected. Now, I would have the degree of vociferation, fuch as *pia- niffimo, piano, forte, fortiffimo*, with all the interme- diate gradations, defignated by the fize of the letters which compofe the emphatic words; and for this, the various fpecies of types from

Pearl

up to

# Five line Pica

will afford an ample fcale.

The ingenious authors of advertifements have, I confefs, in fome degree anticipated my device. We often fee

***Stop Thief! Stop Thief!***

bawled out in

*Double Pica Italics.*

The name of a fhip to be fold, or fome choice arti- cle to be difpofed of, in

English Roman.

And, as a further enforcement of attention, I have feen the figure of a hand with a crier's bell in the act of ringing, advertifing an auction of houfhold furni- ture: every one ftriving to be heard in preference, by a fuperior magnitude of types. At prefent there is none roars out in louder or blacker characters than the Printers themfelves for

## Rags.

There is no looking at the firft page of the Daily Advertifer, without imagining a number of people hallowing and bawling to you to buy their goods or

## Canon.

It follows of courfe, that writers of great irafcibility fhould be charged higher for a work of the fame length, than meek authors; on account of the extra- ordinary fpace their performances muft neceffarily occupy; for thefe gigantic, wrathful types, like ran- ters on the ftage, muft have fufficient elbow room.

For example——Suppofe a newfpaper quarrel to happen between * M and L—M begins the attack pretty fmartly in

Long Primer.

L replies in

Pica Roman.

M advances to

### Great Primer.

L retorts in

### Double Pica.

And fo the conteft fwells to

# Rafcal, Villain, Coward

in five line Pica; which indeed is as far as the art of printing, or a modern quarrel can well go.

A philofophical reafon might be given to prove that large types will more forcibly affect the optic nerve than thofe of a fmaller fize, and are therefore naturally expreffive of energy and vigour. But I leave this difcuffion for the amufement of the gen- tlemen lately elected into our philofophical fociety. It is fufficient for me, if my fyftem fhould be found to be juftified by experience and fact, to which I ap- peal.

I recollect a cafe in point——Some few years be- fore the war, the people of a weftern county, known by the name of *Paxton Boys*, affembled, on account of fome difcontent, in great numbers, and came down with hoftile intentions againft the peace of go- vernment, and with a particular view to fome lead- ing men in the city. *Sir John St. Clair*, who had affumed military command for defence of the city, met one of the obnoxious perfons in the ftreet, and

page of the fheet. When they have proceeded in this alphabetical numeration as far as the letter O, they are fure to fend the author a proof fheet with an

as big as a dollar, to exprefs that the fatigue and la- bour they have gone through is fo great as to make them cry aloud for fome gratuitous refrefhment.

It was referved for me to improve thefe hints in- to a fyftem of general utility. It is indeed high time that fuch a fyftem fhould have been formed. For what alas! are a few CAPITALS and *Italics* in the hands of a vigorous author?——and yet thefe are the only typographical emphatics hitherto in ufe. In perfo- nal altercation, nature has furnifhed ample means of expreffion——the mufcles of the face,——the moti- on of the eyes——the action of the body, the limbs, and even the hands and fingers, all unite in making manifeft the feelings of the foul. Let art do the beft fhe can in cafes where thefe natural figns of fentiment cannot be exhibited.

It is truly lamentable, and has given me much con- cern to obferve with what languor a late religious difpute, and alfo a late law-controverfy have been conducted——not for want of a proper fpirit in the combatants, but merely for want of a fufficient vehi- cle for refentment and rage.

For thefe reafons I have no doubt but that my fcheme of improvement in the art of printing will prove very acceptable to gentlemen difputants, and no lefs fo to the gentlemen printers; as the one will find a new and comprehenfive field opened for the exhi- bition of their refined fentiments, exquifite fenfibili- ties and energy of thought; and the other derive no fmall emolument from the advanced prices which they may reafonably charge for printing the contro- verfial effays, and vigorous effufions of men of fpirit and polite education.

I am, I confefs, fo highly pleafed with my project, that I heartily wifh fome quarrel may foon take place, and fwell even as high as

# Five line Pica

that the utility of my difcovery may be fully mani- fefted. Juft as Mr. —— of the Humane Society anxioufly waited, and, as I believe, fecretly wifhed, that an accident might happen, to evince the efficacy of a grappel he had contrived for difcovering and drawing up drowned bodies.

Left, however, fuch a quarrel fhould not fpeedily occur——

### I hereby give public notice,

(in Englifh Roman No. 1.) that having nothing elfe to do, and having no wife or child to lament the con- fequences of my folly, I propofe to take up any gen- tleman's difcontent, animofity or affront, and to car- ry the fame, in a public conteft with his adverfary as far as

### Great Primer,

or even

## French Canon;

but not farther, without the fpecial leave of the ori- ginal proprietor of the quarrel. Provided however

good becaufe they are rich, appear with the enchanting fimplicity, and charm every behol

L O N D O N,

May 8. The Northerly States of the Ameri republic have adopted fome wife and judicious l that might be a pattern truly worthy example in kingdoms. Thofe in particular for reftraining rafh, though falfely called ' honorable,' practi duelling, and the keeping the Sabbath as a d holy reft, peculiarly deferve a tribute of approba

May 9. It is a fact, that the natural broth a very great man, and a defcendant of the family, is at this moment a prifoner in Maid jail. Nothing can do greater honour to the B laws than that their operations are fuperior t rank and influence whatever.

*Account of the burning of the Montague, Capt. Th Brittell, drawn up by Mr. James Elliott, wh longed to her, and was on board when the acc happened. Dated from on board the Rodney.*

" December 6, 1785, as we lay at Diar Point, about 70 miles below Calcutta, we had t in four thoufand one hundred bags of of falt-p and were ftowing them: the caulker's mate wa ing to heat pitch upon the upper deck, to pa work; he called down the fore-hatchway, t gunner's boy, to hand him up fome fire, up fmall fhovel of the armourer's, to make a fire i forge, to heat the pitch; the boy handing th up the fore-hatchway (the fore-hatches being laid) let a piece of the fire fall down upon the petre; one of the bags having burft, there was falt-petre in the fquare of the hatch-way, which mediately caught fire. We attempted to fmothe but the flames increafed fo faft, that we coul ftay above three minutes in the hold after the took. Mr. Benger the chief officer, came down the hold, but was forced to go up again immed ly. Our cutter and yawl were hawled on fh and the long boat was a-ground in Diamond C I came up out of the hold with the chief officer went into the ftern gallery to look for a boat third officer was then almoft along-fide the Du with fome men in the jolly boat. Perceiving was no affiftance near, I left Mr. Benger in the gallery, and got out of one of the quarter-ports, the mizen chain, and jumped over-board; w fwam under the ftern. Mr. Benger was hangin by a rope, which he quitted, and immediatel fhip blew up. I never faw any more of Mr. ger. Mr. Williams, the third officer, picked in the jolly-boat, with a great many more. not above 50 yards from the fhip when fhe ble From the firft of her taking fire till the explo did not exceed five minutes. Were loft, Mr. Be the chief officer; Mr. M'Intofh, the fifth of Mr. Simfon, furgeon's mate; Mr. Wier, Mr. cent Williams, Mr. Collins, Mr. Cumberland, fhipmen; Mr. Sangfter, gunner; and 25 fore men."

We hear that the reverend Doctor Taylor great friend of Doctor Johnfon, is about to p an effay on the immortality of the foul; a work confirmed the celebrated moralift in opinions, he for fome time doubted.

It is reported in Dublin, that Mr. Pitt in paying a vifit fhortly to that city.

*Tar and feathers* have lately rifen confiderab bove *par* in the metropolis of a neighbouring door.

May 10. Among the various circumftances will ferve in the hands of future hiftorians, to the character of the king of Pruffia, none will more ftriking than this, that in old age, wh infirmities of that period were heaped upon his and his life hung in fufpence in the hands of his ficians, fo vigorous was his genius, and fo pow the terror of his name, that Germany, and the bouring nations, though armed and prepare hoftilities, kept profound filence and peace.

*Extract of a letter from Chefter, May 4.*

" Our county gaol furnifhes the following fin inftances of longevity: The ages of three pe confined for debt amount exactly to 288 years the united ages of fix others are 366. One of poor people has been in prifon 22 years, and others from three to five each. Myfterious, fu is that policy which dooms to perpetual impr ment perfons whofe only crime is poverty! England, fays Voltaire, if a poor fellow cannot dily pay a little money which his hands are at libe the better to enable him to do it, they load him handcuffs!"—Well might our laws refpecting ors draw this farcafm from the French wit."

On Wednefday was married at Manchefter, John Hardman, mafter of the Pack horfe in him, to Mrs. Sarah Wealfon, of the fame p What is remarkable there attended at the cerem an uncle and an aunt, a father and a mother, a ther and a fifter, a fon and a daughter, a man his wife, a fervant and the mafter, together wit miftrefs, bride and bridegroom, and yet all but perfons.

May 12. Wednefday died fuddenly, in the year of his age, at Rotherhithe, captain Ga Beavis, formerly in the Leghorn trade.

May 13. A fhort time fince died at Derby, 75th year of her age, Mrs. Orlando Brown, of the great fir Ifaac Newton, who bequeathe his picture, and the only one he ever fat for, by fir Godfrey Kneller; likewife 2000l.

May 22. By emancipating the minds of th rifians from the enthufiafm of the Church of R a fpirit of licentioufnefs, as it is called in the trary ftates, naturally refults from it. The p France grows more free and fpirited every day no fmall alarm has lately been given to that go ment, in confequence of the multitude of libels

*The Art of Paper War*

*Page 2 of the Pennsylvania Packet, 2 August 1786.*

English Roman.

And, as a further enforcement of attention, I have seen the figure of a hand with a crier's bell in the act of ringing, advertising an auction of houshold furniture: every one striving to be heard in preference, by a superior magnitude of types. At present there is none roars out in louder or blacker characters than the Printers themselves for

# Rags.

There is no looking at the first page of the Daily Advertiser, without imagining a number of people hallowing and bawling to you to buy their goods or lands, to charter their ships, or to let you know that a servant or horse hath strayed away. For my part, I am so possessed with this idea, that as soon as I take up the paper of the day, I turn over to articles of intelligence as quick as possible, lest my eyes should be stunned with the ocular uproar of the first page. For I am a peaceable man, and hate nothing more than the confused noise of a mob.

My project, then, consists in this, that the printer, in composing any work, should adapt the size of his types to the spirit of the author, so that a reader may become in a degree personally acquainted with a writer whilst he is perusing his work. Thus, an author of cool and equable spirits might take

Burgeois Roman

for his medium, and would probably never rise higher than

Great Primer;

whilst a passionate man, engaged in a warm controversy, would thunder vengeance in

# French Canon.

It follows of course, that writers of great irascibility should be charged higher for a work of the same length, than meek authors; on account of the extraordinary space their performances must necessarily occupy; for these gigantic, wrathful types, like ranters on the stage, must have sufficient elbow room.

For example—Suppose a newspaper quarrel to happen between *M and L[2]—M begins the attack pretty smartly in

Long Primer.

L replies in

Pica Roman.

M advances to

Great Primer.

L retorts in

Double Pica.

And so the contest swells to

# Rascal,
# Coward,
# Villain,

2. Note in Original: "Lest some ill-disposed person should misapply those initials, I think proper to declare, that M signifies Merchant, and L Lawyer." Of course they also signify Moore and Lewis.

in five line Pica; which indeed is as far as the art of printing, or a modern quarrel can well go.

A philosophical reason might be given to prove that large types will more forcibly affect the optic nerve than those of a smaller size, and are therefore naturally expressive of energy and vigour. But I leave this discussion for the amusement of the gentlemen lately elected into our philosophical society. It is sufficient for me, if my system should be found to be justified by experience and fact, to which I appeal.

I recollect a case in point.—Some few years before the war, the people of a western country, known by the name of *Paxton Boys*, assembled, on account of some discontent, in great numbers, and came down with hostile intentions against the peace of government, and with a particular view to some leading men in the city.[3] *Sir John St. Clair*, who had assumed military command for defence of the city, met one of the obnoxious persons in the street, and told him that he had seen the manifesto of the insurgents, and that his name was particularized in letters *as long as his fingers*. The gentleman immediately packed up his most valuable effects, and sent them with his family into Jersey for security. Had Sir John only said that he had seen his name mentioned in the manifesto, it is probable he would not have been so seriously alarmed; but the unusual size of the letters was to him a plain indication that the insurgents were determined to carry their revenge to a proportionable extremity.

I could confirm my system by innumerable instances in fact and practice. The title-page of every book is a proof in point. It announces the subject treated of in conspicuous characters; as if the author stood at the door of his edifice, calling to every one to enter in and partake of the entertainment he has prepared; and

3. In Winter 1764–65, irate at Quaker beneficence to Indians, frontiersmen calling themselves the Paxton Boys massacred a dozen Indians being held in protective custody at Lancaster jail. Threatening like vengeance on Indians protected in barracks at Philadelphia, but turned back by armed citizens, the Paxtons sent a remonstrance naming a "J. P." (James Pemberton) as leader of the obnoxious society that "had abetted our Indian Enemies" (*Colonial Records*, 9:141).

some even scream out their invitation in red letters. The journeymen printers have also a custom founded on the same principles. They distinguish every sheet of printing by a letter of the alphabet, which may be seen at the bottom of the first page of the sheet. When they have proceeded in this alphabetical numeration as far as the letter O, they are sure to send the author a proof sheet with an

# O

as big as a dollar, to express that the fatigue and labour they have gone through is so great as to make them cry aloud for some gratuitous refreshment.

It was reserved for me to improve these hints into a system of general utility. It is indeed high time that such a system should have been formed. For what alas! are a few CAPITALS and *Italics* in the hands of a vigorous author?—and yet these are the only typographical emphatics hitherto in use. In personal altercation, nature has furnished ample means of expression—the muscles of the face,—the motion of the eyes—the action of the body, the limbs, and even the hands and fingers, all unite in making manifest the feelings of the soul. Let art do the best she can in cases where these natural signs of sentiment cannot be exhibited.

It is truly lamentable, and has given me much concern to observe with what languor a late religious dispute, and also a late law-controversy have been conducted[4]—not for want of a proper spirit in the combatants, but merely for want of a sufficient vehicle for resentments and rage.

For these reasons I have no doubt but that my scheme of im-

---

4. During June and July the *Packet* had printed two exchanges of letters on religious and legal controversy—about disunity in the Presbyterian Synod and on whether the assembly could legally charter a national bank—both languid relative to the Moore-Lewis exchange.

provement in the art of printing will prove very acceptable to gentlemen disputants, and no less so to the gentlemen printers; as the one will find a new and comprehensive field opened for the exhibition of their refined sentiments, exquisite sensibilities and energy of thought; and the other derive no small emolument from the advanced prices which they may reasonably charge for printing the controversial essays, and vigorous effusions of men of spirit and polite education.

I am, I confess, so highly pleased with my project, that I heartily wish some quarrel may soon take place, and swell even as high as

# Five line Pica

that the utility of my discovery may be fully manifested. Just as Mr. —— of the Humane Society anxiously waited, and, as I believe, secretly wished, that an accident might happen, to evince the efficacy of a grappel he had contrived for discovering and drawing up drowned bodies.[5]

Lest, however, such a quarrel should not speedily occur—

### [I hereby give public notice,]

(in English Roman No. I,) that having nothing else to do, and having no wife or child to lament the consequences of my folly, I propose to take up any gentleman's discontent, animosity or af-

5. Not to be confused with the later Society for the Prevention of Cruelty to Animals, the Philadelphia Humane Society was founded in 1780 to resuscitate victims of drowning or asphyxiation.

front, and to carry the same, in a public contest with his adversary as far as

Great Primer,

or even

# French Canon;

but not farther, without the special leave of the original proprietor of the quarrel. Provided, however, that the dispute began in

Burgeois Roman;

for if it originated only in

Pearl

Non Pareil

or

*Minion*

I shall hardly think it worth my notice. To shew that I am in earnest in this offer, I shall leave my address with the Printers of this essay, that any gentleman quarreller may readily find a champion for the cause which he does not chuse to championize himself.

I anxiously wait the issue of this my proposed scheme, not without some secret hopes that it may prove a lucky hit, and procure me that public renown and popular favour which I have so long in vain laboured to acquire.

PROJECTOR.

*Pennsylvania Packet 2 August 1786.*

## *NITIDIA'S ANSWER*

In the late summer of 1786 a syndicate of publishers designed a monthly magazine for Philadelphia—which had been without one since the *Pennsylvania Magazine* ceased a decade earlier. Their *Colum-*

*bian Magazine* was patterned after London's *Gentleman's Magazine* but strongly emphasized national culture, promising in the preface of its first issue (October) to provide "contemporary evidence of the progress of literature and the arts" in America. Its first editor was one of the proprietors, Matthew Carey. A recent exile from Dublin, he had begun the *Pennsylvania Evening Herald* in January 1785, and now edited the *Columbian* from its first issue through its fifth in February. But by that time he had established another monthly magazine of his own, probably because his anti-Federalist views clashed with those of the other proprietors. His *American Museum* was not intended as a direct competitor, however, but was to specialize in reprinting articles from newspapers that deserved wider circulation and also pamphlets from the war that Carey felt worthy of perpetuating in his columns—among them Hopkinson's "Battle of the Kegs" along with his more recent *Packet* essay on "Whitewashing," both of which appeared in Carey's inaugural issue, January 1787.

Hopkinson himself took over editorship of the *Columbian* during March, April and May, while the proprietors sought a permanent editor. As editor, he fleshed out the "Poetry" department with selections from his own early verse, here signed "H." In the April issue was an original essay in which he assumed the role of an irate housewife replying to the essay on "Whitewashing" that Carey had reprinted. (One measure of the popularity achieved by both essays is that Carey republished them in tandem when he issued a bound third edition of the *Museum* in 1790.)

Sir,

I have seen a piece in Mr. Carey's Museum, upon the subject of *White-Washing*, in which that necessary duty of a good housewife is treated with unmerited ridicule—I should probably have forgotten the foolish thing by this time—but the season coming on, which most women think suitable for cleansing their apartments from the smoak and dirt of the winter, I find this saucy author dish'd up in every family, and his flippant performance quoted wherever a wife attempts to exercise her reasonable prerogative or execute the duties of her station. Women generally employ their time to better purpose than scribbling. The cares and comforts of a family rest principally upon their shoulders—hence it is that there are but few female authors—and the men, knowing how necessary our attentions are to their happiness, take every opportunity of discouraging literary accomplishments in the fair sex. You hear it echoed from every quarter—My wife cannot make verses, it is true; but she makes an excellent pudding—she can't correct the press; but she can correct her children, and scold her servants with admirable discretion—she can't unravel the intricacies of political œconomy and federal government; but she can knit charming stockings—and this they call praising a wife, and doing justice to her good character—with much nonsense of the like kind.—I say, women generally employ their time to better purpose than scribbling; otherwise this facetious writer had not gone so long unanswered.—We have ladies who some times lay down the needle and take up the pen, I wonder none of them have attempted some reply.—For my part I do not pretend to be an author. I never appeared in print in my life; but I can no longer forbear saying something in answer to such impertinence. Only consider, Mr. Editor, our situation. Men are naturally inattentive to the decencies of life—but why I should be so complaisant,—I say, they are naturally nasty beasts: if it were not that their connection with the refined sex, polished their manners, and had a happy influence on the general œconomy of life, these lords of the creation would wallow in filth, and populous cities would infect the atmosphere with their noxious vapours. It is the attention and assiduity of the women that prevent men from degenerating into swine.—How important then are the services we render—and yet for these very services we are made the subject of ridicule and fun—base ingratitude—nauseous creatures!—Perhaps you may think, I am in a passion—No, Mr. Editor, I do assure you I was never more composed in my life—and yet it is enough to provoke a saint to see how unreasonably we are treated by the men.—Why now there's my husband—a good enough sort of a man in the main—but I will give you a small sample of him—He comes into the parlour the other day, where, to be sure, I was cutting up a piece of linen.—Lord, says he, what a clutter here is—I can't bear to see the parlour look like a taylor's shop—besides I am going to make some important philosophical experiments, and must have sufficient room.—You must know, my husband is one of your wou'd-be philosophers,—well, I bundled up my linen as quick as I could, and began to darn a pair of ruffles; which took up no room, and could give no offence—I tho't however, I would watch my lord and master's important business.—In about half an hour the tables were covered with all manner of trumpery—bottles of water, phials of drugs, paste board, paper and cards, glew, paste and gum-arabic, files, knives, scissars, and needles, rosin, wax, silk, thread, rags, jaggs, tags, books, pamphlets and papers. Lord bless me! I am almost out of breath, and yet I have not enumerated half the articles—well—to work he went—and altho' I did not understand the object of his manœuvres, yet I could sufficiently discover that he did not succeed in any one operation—I was glad of that, I confess—and good reason too—For, after he had fatigued himself with mischief, like a monkey in a china shop, and had called the servants to clear every thing away, I took a view of the scene my parlour exhibited—I shall not even attempt a minute description—Suffice it to say that he had overset his ink-stand, and stained my best mahogany table with ink; he had spilt a quantity of vitriol, and burnt a great hole in my carpet; my marble hearth was all over spotted with melted rosin—besides this, he had broken three china cups, four wine glasses, two tumblers, and one of my handsomest decanters—and after all, as I said before, I perceived that he had not succeeded in any one operation.—By the bye,—tell your friend the white-wash scribbler, that this is one means by which our closets become furnished with "halves of China bowls, cracked tumblers, broken wine glasses, tops of tea-pots and stoppers of departed decanters,"—I say, I took a view of the dirt and devastation my philosophic husband had occasioned—and there I sat, like Patience on a monument, smiling at grief—but it worked inwardly—yes, Mr. Editor, it worked inwardly—I would almost as lieve the melted rosin and vitriol had been in his throat, as on my dear marble hearth and my beautiful carpet.—It is not true that women have no power over their own feelings—For notwithstanding this provocation, I said nothing, or next to nothing; for I only observ'd very pleasantly, that a lady of my acquaintance had told me that the reason why philosophers are called *literary* men is, because they make a great *litter*—not a word more—however the servant cleared away, and down sat the philosopher.—A friend dropt in soon after—Your servant, sir, how do you do?—'Oh Lord! *I am almost fatigued to death—I have been all the morning making philosophical experiments.'*—I was now more hardly put to it to smother a laugh, than I had been just before to contain my rage—my *Precious* went out soon after, and I, as you may suppose, mustered all my forces—brushes, buckets, soap, sand, lime-skins, and cocoa-nut shells, with all the powers of housewifery were immediately employed—I was certainly the best philosopher of the two: for my experiments succeeded, and his did not—all was well again, except my poor carpet—my vitriolized carpet—which still remained a mournful memento of philosophic fury, or rather philosophic folly. This operation was scarce over, when in came my experimental philosopher and told me, with all the indifference in the world, that he had invited six gentlemen to dine with him at three o'clock—It was then past one—I complained of the short notice—poh, poh, says he, you can get a leg of mutton and a loin of veal, and a few potatoes, and it will do well enough—Heavens! what a chaos must the head of a philosopher be? a leg of mutton, a loin of veal and potatoes!—I was at a loss whether I should laugh or be angry—but there was no time for determining—I had but an hour and an half to do a world of business in. My carpet, which had suffered in the cause of experimental philosophy in the morning, was destined to be most shamefully dishonoured in the afternoon, by a deluge of nasty tobacco juice—Gentlemen smoakers love segars better than carpets.—Think, Mr. Editor, what a woman must endure under such circumstances, and then, after all, to be reproached with her cleanliness, and to have her white-washings, her scourings and scrubbings made the subject of ridicule—it is more than patience can put up with.—What I have now exhibited is but a small specimen of the injuries we sustain from the boasted superiority of men. But we will not be laughed out of our cleanliness—A woman would rather be called any thing than a *slut*, as a man would rather be thought a knave than a fool.—I had a great deal more to say; but I am called away—we are just preparing to white-wash, and of course I have a deal of business on my hands.—The white-wash buckets are paraded—the brushes are ready—my husband is gone off—so much the better—when one is about a thorough cleaning—the first dirty thing to be removed is one's husband—I am called for again—Adieu.

Yours
NITIDIA

*Columbian Magazine, 1 (April 1787), 375–77.*

# FOR THE FEDERALIST PRESS (1787-1788)

During the summer of 1787, Congress sponsored a Constitutional Convention sitting in Philadelphia to revise the ten-year-old Articles of Confederation that had been found inadequate to the needs or survival of a developing nation, since they included no provisions for regulating internal finance or external commerce or even exercising executive functions. The representatives emerged from the summer's secret sessions with much more than a revision. They proposed a radically new form of government. Published 17 September, the proposed Constitution featured an innovative system of checks and balances in a federal structure that nicely distinguished between state and federal powers while providing for a strong executive chosen by the people, a legislature accountable to the people, and an independent judiciary monitoring the other branches for the people. Ten days later, on 27 September, Congress directed that the document be submitted to the states for ratification.

In Pennsylvania, the state convention convened on 21 November, with popularly elected representatives in the proportion of two to one favoring the Constitution. Nevertheless, the debates dragged on for three weeks because George Bryan's (now misnamed) Constitutionalists tried to delay and subvert the inevitable dissolution of their own state constitution that for a decade had given them political power out of proportion to their numbers. Initially they obstructed proceedings by refusing to attend, thus depriving the convention of a quorum, but state officials and a restive mob persuaded recalcitrant absentees to return. For the rest of the session, then, Bryan's people used parliamentary tactics and fierce oratory to delay ratification, and thereby encourage their counterparts in such states as New York where popular sentiment was less favorable to the Constitution.

In Pennsylvania, the opposition now lay almost entirely in the outlying farming and frontier communities whose citizens saw the struggle as still another threat from aristocratic merchant-bankers in the city. The anti-Federalist leaders in the convention, though now shrewd politicians and astute lawyers, flaunted their occupational backgrounds —William Findley had been bred to the weaver's trade and John Smilie to the carpenter's. They focused their attacks on the personality of the Federalist leader James Wilson, whose bearing if not background had been aristocratic, and accused him of acting in secrecy, duplicity, deception, and especially undue haste that showed consummate contempt for the people's capability to deliberate on the issues.

The irony in this attack was that Wilson, as representative to the national convention, had been the architect of the Constitution's democratic base. But he had also led the state Republican party's attacks on George Bryan's power over the past decade, and the ratification issue now raised their conflict to a national stage. Besides the parliamentary maneuvering of Findley and Smilie, Bryan also used the press to turn public opinion against Wilson's arguments, most effectively through a series of essays signed "Centinel," widely reprinted in broadsides and newspapers—both Federalist and anti-Federalist. The essays sometimes argued issues in the manner of the Hamilton-Madison-Jay Federalist papers, but sometimes they merely rang changes on such charges as "treason," "aristocrats," "traitors," "tyranny," and "tories."

Amidst these echoes from the turbulent mid-Seventies, Hopkinson leaped into the skirmish with a political allegory slightly reminiscent of his celebrated *Pretty Story* but lacking narrative thrust or the dispassionate irony that had made the earlier fable effective. "The New Roof" featured in the *Packet* for 29 December disintegrated to invective against a writer, "Pennsylvaniensis," who had dared suspect General Washington's patriotism. Still, in using the analogy of building a roof, Hopkinson turned John Smilie's flaunted carpentry against him and provided Federalists with a popular symbol of the Constitution.

# *THE NEW ROOF*

The roof of a certain mansion house was observed to be in a very bad condition, and insufficient for the purpose of protection from the inclemencies of the weather. This was matter of surprize and speculation, as it was well known the roof was not more than 12 years old, and therefore, its defects could not be ascribed to a natural decay by time. Altho' there were many different opinions as to the cause of this deficiency, yet all agreed that the family could not sleep in comfort or safety under it. It was at last determined to appoint some skilful architects to survey and examine the defective roof, to make report of its condition, and to point out such alterations and repairs as might be found necessary. These skilful architects, accordingly went into a thorough examination of the faulty roof, and found

1st. That the whole frame was too weak.

2d. That there were indeed 13 rafters, but that these rafters were not connected by any braces or ties, so as to form a union of strength.

3d. That some of these rafters were thick and heavy, and others very slight, and as the whole had been put together whilst the timber was yet green, some had warped outwards, and of course sustained an undue weight, whilst others warping inwards, had shrunk from bearing any weight at all.

4th. That the lathing and shingling had not been secured with iron nails, but only wooden pegs, which, shrinking and swelling by successions of wet and dry weather, had left the shingles so loose, that many of them had been blown away by the winds, and that before long, the whole would probably, in like manner, be blown away.

5th. That the cornice was so ill proportioned, and so badly put up, as to be neither of use, nor an ornament. And

6th. That the roof was so flat as to admit the most idle servants in the family, their playmates and acquaintance to trample on and abuse it.

Having made these observations, these judicious architects gave it as their opinion, that it would be altogether vain and fruitless to attempt any alterations or amendments in a roof so defective in all points; and therefore proposed to have it entirely removed, and that a new roof of a better construction should be erected over the mansion house. And they also prepared and offered a drawing or plan of a new roof, such as they thought most excellent for security, duration, and ornament. In forming this plan they consulted the most celebrated authors in ancient and modern architecture, and brought into their plan the most approved parts, according to their judgments, selected from the models before them; and finally endeavoured to proportion the whole to the size of the building, and strength of the walls.

This proposal of a new roof, it may well be supposed, became the principal subject of conversation in the family, and the opinions upon it were various according to the judgment, interest, or ignorance of the disputants.

On a certain day, the servants of the family had assembled in the great hall to discuss this important point; amongst these was James the architect, who had been one of the surveyors of the old roof, and had a principal hand in forming the plan of a new one.[1] A great number of the tenants had also gathered out of doors and crowded the windows and avenues to the hall, which were left open that they might hear the arguments for and against the new roof.

Now there was an old woman, known by the name of Margery, who had got a comfortable apartment in the mansion house.[2] This woman was of an intriguing spirit, of a restless and inveterate temper, fond of tattle, and a great mischief maker. In this situation, and with these talents, she unavoidably acquired an influence in the family, by the exercise of which, according to her natural propensity, she had long kept the house in confusion, and sown discord and discontent amongst the servants. Margery was, for many reasons, an irreconcileable enemy to the new roof, and to the architects who had planned it; amongst these, two reasons

---

1. Member of the Second Continental Congress as well as of the Constitutional Convention, James Wilson had been Hopkinson's attorney during his impeachment in 1780.
2. George Bryan had been called "Margery the Midwife" by the *Independent Gazetteer* before that paper became a leading spokesman for the anti-Federalists; the subsequent allusion to Margery's "old red cloak" is to his decision that judges should wear scarlet rather than black robes (April 1785).

were obvious—1st, The mantle piece on which her cups and platters were placed, was made of a portion of the great cornice, and she boiled her pot with the shingles that blew off from the defective roof: And 2dly, It so happened that in the construction of the new roof, her apartment would be considerably lessened. No sooner, therefore, did she hear of the plan proposed by the architects, but she put on her old red cloak, and was day and night trudging amongst the tenants and servants, and crying out against the new roof and the framers of it. Amongst these she had selected William, Jack, and Robert, three of the tenants, and instigated them to oppose the plan in agitation[3]—she caused them to be sent to the great hall on the day of debate, and furnished them with innumerable alarms and fears, cunning arguments, and specious objections.

Now the principal arguments and objections with which Margery had instructed William, Jack, and Robert, were,

1st. That the architects had not exhibited a bill of scantling for the new roof, as they ought to have done; and therefore the carpenters, under pretence of providing timber for it, might lay waste whole forests, to the ruin of the farm.[4]

2nd. That no provision was made in the plan for a trap door for the servants to pass through with water, if the chimney should take fire; and that, in case of such an accident, it might hereafter be deemed penal to break a hole in the roof for access to save the whole building from destruction.

3d. That this roof was to be guarded by battlements, which, in stormy seasons would prove dangerous to the family, as the bricks might be blown down and fall on their heads.

4th. It was observed that the old roof was ornamented with 12 pedestals ranged along the ridge, which were objects of universal admiration; whereas, according to the new plan, these pedestals were only to be placed along the eves of the roof, over the walls;

---

3. William Findley, John Smilie, and Robert Whitehill.
4. Symbols in the ensuing paragraphs are: bill of scantling—bill of rights; trap door—freedom of the press; battlements—standing army; and the twelve pedestals—trial by jury.

and that a cupola was to supply their place on the ridge or summit of the new roof.—As to the cupola itself, some of the objecters said it was too heavy and would become a dangerous burthen to the building, whilst others alledged that it was too light and would certainly be blown away by the wind.

5th. It was insisted that the 13 rafters being so strongly braced together, the individual and separate strength of each rafter would be lost in the compounded and united strength of the whole; and so the roof might be considered as one solid mass of timber, and not as composed of distinct rafters, like the old roof.

6th. That according to the proposed plan, the several parts of the roof were so framed as to mutually strengthen and support each other, and therefore, there was great reason to fear that the whole might stand independent of the walls; and that in time the walls might crumble away, and the roof remain suspended in air, threatening destruction to all that should come under it.

To these objections, James the architect, in substance, replied,

1st. As to the want of a bill of scantling, he observed, that if the timber for this roof was to be purchased from a stranger, it would have been quite necessary to have such a bill, lest the stranger should charge in account more than he was entitled to; but as the timber was to be cut from our own lands, a bill of scantling was both useless and improper—of no use, because the wood always was and always would be the property of the family, whether growing in the forest, or fabricated into a roof for the mansion house—and improper, because the carpenters would be bound by the bill of scantling, which, if it should not be perfectly accurate, a circumstance hardly to be expected, either the roof would be defective for want of sufficient materials, or the carpenters must cut from the forest without authority, which is penal by the laws of the house.

To the second objection he said, that a trap door was not properly a part in the frame of a roof; but there could be no doubt but that the carpenters would take care to have such a door through the shingling, for the family to carry water through, dirty or clean, to extinguish fire, either in the chimney or on the roof; and that this was the only proper way of making such a door.

3d. As to the battlements, he insisted that they were absolutely necessary for the protection of the whole house.—1st. In case of an attack by robbers, the family would defend themselves behind these battlements, and annoy and disperse the enemy.—2dly. If any of the adjoining buildings should take fire, the battlements would screen the roof from the destructive flames: and 3dly. They would retain the rafters in their respective places in case any of them should from rottenness or warping be in danger of falling from the general union, and injuring other parts of the roof; observing that the battlements should always be ready for these purposes, as there would be neither time or opportunity for building them after an assault was actually made, or a conflagration begun. As to the bricks being blown down, he said the whole was in the power of the family to repair or remove any loose or dangerous parts, and there could be no doubt but that their vigilance would at all times be sufficient to prevent accidents of this kind.

4th. With respect to the 12 pedestals he acknowledged their use and elegance; but observed that these, like all other things, were only so in their proper places, and under circumstances suited to their nature and design, and insisted that the ridge of a roof was not the place for pedestals, which should rest on the solid wall, being made of the same materials and ought in propriety to be considered as so many projections or continuations of the wall itself, and not as component parts of the wooden roof. As to the cupola, he said that all agreed there should be one of some kind or other, as well for a proper finish to the building, as for the purposes of indicating the winds and containing a bell to sound an alarm in cases of necessity. The objections to the present cupola, he said, were too contradictory to merit a reply.

To the 5th objection he answered, That the intention really was to make a firm and substantial roof by uniting the strength of the 13 rafters; and that this was so far from annihilating the several rafters and rendering them of no use individually, that it was manifest from a bare inspection of the plan, that the strength of each contributed to the strength of the whole, and that the existence of each and all were essentially necessary to the existence of the whole fabric as a roof.

Lastly. He said, that the roof was indeed so framed that the parts should mutually support and check each other, but it was most absurd and contrary to the known laws of nature, to infer from thence that the whole frame should stand self supported in air, for however its component parts might be combined with respect to each other, the whole must necessarily rest upon and be supported by the walls. That the walls might indeed stand for a few years in a ruinous and uninhabitable condition without any roof, but the roof could not for a moment stand without the support of the walls; and finally, that of all dangers and apprehensions this of the roof's remaining when the walls are gone was the most absurd and impossible.

It was mentioned before, that, whilst this debate was carrying on in the great hall, the windows and doors were crowded with attendants. Amongst these was a half crazy fellow who was suffered to go at large because he was a harmless lunatic.[5] Margery, however, thought he might be a serviceable engine in promoting opposition to the new roof. As people of deranged understandings are easily irritated, she exasperated this poor fellow against the architects, and fill'd him with the most terrible apprehensions from the new roof; making him believe that the architects had provided a dark hole in the garret, where he was to be chained for life. Having by these suggestions filled him with rage and terror, she let him loose among the crowd, where he roar'd and bawl'd to the annoyance of all bye-standers. This circumstance would not have been mentioned but for the opportunity of exhibiting the stile and manner in which a deranged and irritated

5. Hopkinson thought that articles in the *Independent Gazetteer* signed "Philadelphiensis" were by Benjamin Workman, recently transplanted from Dublin, a teacher of navigation and astronomy and later author of popular textbooks on gauging, accounting, and geography as well as several almanacs.

mind will express itself—one of his rhapsodies shall conclude this narrative.—[6]

"The new Roof! the new Roof! Oh! the new Roof!—Shall demagogues, despising every sense of order and decency, frame a new roof?—If such bare-faced presumption, arrogance and tyrannical proceeding will not rouse you, the goad and the whip—the goad and the whip should do it—but you are careless and insecure sinners, whom neither admonitions, entreaties and threatnings can reclaim—sinners consigned to unutterable and endless woe—Where is that pusillanimous wretch who can submit to such contumely—oh the *ultima Ratio Regium:* [He got these three Latin words from Margery] oh the *ultima Ratio Regium*—ah! the days of Nero! ah! the days of Caligula! ah! the British tyrant and his infernal junto—glorious revolution—awful crisis—self-important nabobs—diabolical plots and secret machinations—oh the architects! the architects—they have seized the government, secured power, brow beat with insolence and assume majesty—oh the architects! they will treat you as conquered slaves—they will make you pass under the yoke, and leave their gluttony and riot to attend the pleasing sport—oh that the glory of the Lord may be made perfect—that he would shew strength with his arm and scatter the proud in the imaginations of their hearts—blow the trumpet—sound an alarm—I will cry day and night—behold is not this my number five—attend to my words ye women labouring of child—ye sick persons and young children—behold—behold the lurking places, the despots, the infernal designs—lust of dominion and conspiracies—from battle and murder and from sudden death—good Lord deliver us.

"Figure to yourselves, my good fellows, a man with a cow and a horse—oh the battlements, the battlements, they will fall upon

---

6. The concluding paragraphs are a pastiche of quotations largely wrenched out of the context of the fifth "Philadelphiensis" essay appearing on 19 December 1787; e.g., where the expression here is "you are careless and insecure sinners" "Philadelphiensis" had written, "Your condition must be like that of the insecure sinner."

his cow, they will fall upon his horse, and wound them, and bruise them and kill them, and the poor man will perish with hunger. Do I exaggerate?—no truly—Europe and Asia and Indostan deny it if you can—oh God! what a monster is man!—A being possessed of knowledge, reason, judgment and an immortal soul—what a monster is man! But the architects are said to be men of skill—then the more their shame—curse on the villains!—they are despots, sycophants, Jesuits, tories, lawyers—curse on the villains! We beseech thee to hear us—Lord have mercy on us—Oh!—Ah! —Ah!—Oh!—"

*Pennsylvania Packet 29 December 1787.*

# OBJECTIONS TO PROPOSED PLAN

During January 1788, the *Independent Gazetteer* published a series of letters commenting on "an *extraordinary* meeting" of "aristocrats" at a local tavern where James Wilson had called for renewed vigor in raising money for pro-Federalist propaganda. "Tom Peep, Junior" asserted that the two thousand pounds goal was intended for bribery as well as propaganda (14 January). A month later, the *Pennsylvania Gazette* published Hopkinson's unsigned report of an extraordinary meeting among anti-Federalists. These were prisoners in the City Jail, most of them bearing Scotch-Irish names, and all members of the "Wheelbarrow Society," so-called because under an act of 1787 the city employed them (under guard) as street cleaners whose equipment included wheelbarrows.

OBJECTIONS *to the proposed Plan of Government for the United States, on GENUINE PRINCIPLES.*

At a Meeting of the *Wheel-barrow Society,* in the Prison-yard, Philadelphia, February the 8th, 1788.

Present fifty-eight members.

JEM DORAN in the Chair.

After mature discussion, the Society unanimously agreed in the following

FUNDAMENTAL PRINCIPLES.

1st. *Pure natural liberty* is the right of every man to do whatever he pleases *without controul,* and to possess, *without retribution,* whatever he can acquire by *valour* or *address.*

2d. States or sovereign powers are as individuals in a state of nature; and therefore true political liberty, or the liberty of a state as a body politic, is the right of that state, or of those who are in the possession of the sovereignty thereof, to do such things and enact such laws, as may be thought conducive to the advancement of the powers and interests of that state, or of the government thereof, uncontrouled by the artificial system of restraints, known by the name of *The Law of Nations.*

3d. All systems of government, whether operating on states or on individuals, although ostensibly formed and specially declared to be for the establishment of general justice and of general good, are, in fact, systems of coercion, restraint and oppression, and ought to be abhorred by the true sons of freedom as invasions and abridgements of their natural rights.

4th. Whereas, in the present imperfect state of things, *true natural liberty,* as defined in our first fundamental principle, cannot be universally enjoyed, necessity enforces a submission to what is called government, under some form or other.

5th. According to the foregoing principles, that form of government is the best, which contains the fewest restraints, and leaves in the hands of the governed the greatest portion of natural liberty, and the fullest scope for the exercise of personal prowess and native ingenuity; it being demonstrable, that if the component parts of any society are left free, and become, *by any means,* rich and happy, the whole of that society will be free, rich and happy.

6th. The worst of all possible governments is that, which, by the vigorous operation of general laws, and a complication of internal checks, restraints and regulations, prevents individual states or persons from prosecuting their separate interests in their own way; most wickedly sacrificing the emolument of individuals to what is called the glory and prosperity of the whole.

These fundamental principles being established, the plan of

government proposed by the late General Convention for the United States was taken up, considered by paragraphs, and compared with the doctrines laid down; and after some debate, the following resolutions were unanimously adopted, viz.

1st. *Resolved,* That the constitution proposed for the United States is a *consolidated government,* pregnant with the seeds of coercion and restraint, and therefore a system of tyranny and oppression.

2d. *Resolved,* That under such a government, neither states nor individuals can do or refuse to do what they please, in all cases, which is a direct infringement of the natural liberty of both, as defined in our first fundamental principle.

3d. *Resolved,* That under such a government men of education, abilities and property, commonly called *the well born,* will be most likely to get into places of power and trust, to the exclusion of a large majority of a contrary description.

4th. *Resolved,* That as this constitution most arbitrarily and inhumanly prohibits the emission of paper money, and other resources by which the unfortunate debtor may throw off the discouraging burthen of his obligations, it ought to be considered, as in fact it is, a system of tyranny and oppression, compelling citizens in many instances to do things extremely disagreeable, and contrary to their interest.

5th. *Resolved,* That under such a government the industrious and wealthy may enjoy their property in security, to the great injury of those who have no property at all.

6th. *Resolved,* That under such a government there will be no encouragement for gentlemen of adventure and address to procure subsistance and wealth by extraordinary modes of acquirement, because what is called the vigour of law will pervade the whole union.

7th. *Resolved,* That the government proposed is consonant with our 6th fundamental principle, and the worst of all possible governments; and therefore

8th. *Resolved,* That the members of the late general convention, who framed, voted for, and recommended this plan of government, and all state conventions who have or shall hereafter adopt and ratify the same, and all those individuals, who, by word of mouth, by writing and publishing, or by any other means, shall express their approbation of the said infamous constitution, are, and ought to be, considered by all the true sons of liberty as demagogues, aristocratics, conspirators, traytors, tyrants, and enemies of the natural rights of mankind.

9th. *Resolved,* That as we are the most numerous and respectable body that have as yet combined, formally to avow and publish a disapprobation of this new constitution, it is fit and proper that we should be regularly organized, that other worthy malcontents in this and other states may, by association or election, be annexed to our community, and so make up a union of strength to oppose the establishment of this tyrannical government: Therefore,

10th. *Resolved,* That we will now proceed to the election of a President, Vice-President and Secretary.

Whereupon, the ballots being fairly taken and counted, stood as follows:

*For the* PRESIDENTSHIP.

| | |
|---|---|
| For the Author of the pieces signed *Centinel,* | 51 votes. |
| For Jem Doran, — — — | 5 |
| For Arthur McGarity, — — — | 2 |

VICE-PRESIDENT.

| | |
|---|---|
| For L________ M________, Esquire, of Maryland, — — — | 47 votes.[1] |
| For Daniel Cronan, — — — | 8 |
| For Pat Dalton, — — — | 3 |

SECRETARY.

| | |
|---|---|
| For the Author of the pieces signed *Philadelphiensis,* — — — | 30 votes. |
| For Kit Carbery, — — — | 28[2] |

1. In the *Independent Gazette* for 5 February, "Centinel, No. XIV" gave extracts from a pamphlet by Luther Martin, one of Maryland's delegates, as confirmation that the Federalists had railroaded the Constitution through the Convention.
2. Captain Carberry, notorious "deranged" leader of the troops that had marched on Congress in 1783, had been extradited from his refuge in Maryland the following year, and found guilty of insurrection.

The following members were then appointed a committee of correspondence, viz. Jem Doran, Arthur McGarity, John Doughty, Pat Dalton, Daniel Cronan, James Bulger, and Kit Carbery, to hold communication with the late adherents of General Shays in the state of Massachusetts,[3] and with other worthy opposers in the several states.

The society directed that these their proceedings should be made public, and then resumed their daily occupation of cleaning the streets and common sewers.

*Pennsylvania Gazette 20 February 1788.*

# *DISEASES OF THE MIND*

During the winter of 1787–88, Hopkinson was publishing satires against the anti-Federalists once a month. Then in mid-March, stung by vicious attacks against his idols Washington and Franklin, he wrote for the *Independent Gazetteer* three columns of direct invective at Benjamin Workman, naming him as "Philadelphiensis"—"sculking behind assumed signatures" as a tool of the anti-Federalist conspiracy, pouring "torrents of personal abuse and opprobrious slander against men of high esteem" (11 March 1788). Hopkinson himself signed his letter with an assumed name, "A. B.," and the editor, Eleazar Oswald, added a note that the author's offer to pay for its insertion was hereby accepted ("eleven squares at a dollar [about $11.00 in today's money] a square, specie"), with the proceeds going to the Overseers of the Poor so that nobody would think that the opinions expressed or implied by the writer were anyone's but his own.

In the same columns ten days later, Workman announced that he was preparing a reply to Hopkinson's letter. But before he could publish it, "Centinel" rose to his defense. Concluding an exposé of a grand Federalist conspiracy to defraud the public, "Centinel" cited Hopkinson as a typical tool: "The scurrilous attack of the *little Fiddler* upon

---

3. In August 1786, ex-Captain Daniel Shays marshaled a group of desperate farmers in Western Massachusetts to protest the legislature's failure to issue paper money that would have eased their debts. Numbering 1200, the group had dwindled to 150 by February when they were captured by Benjamin Lincoln. Shays fled to Vermont under sentence of death—until pardoned in June 1788.

Mr. Workman . . . is characteristical of the man; he has ever been the base parasite and tool of the wealthy and great" (24 March). "Centinel" warned that if he were not more cautious, the world would be reminded that "Little Francis" had a sordid skeleton in his closet —"the suit of clothes, and the quarter cask of wine, will not be forgot."

Two days later came the first of Workman's own two-part reply, protesting his innocence of Hopkinson's "malicious, cruel, and unprovoked" allegations, and calling them the production of a parasite and mean bully employed by a declining party grasping at any straw for revenge. The next week, he concluded by echoing "Centinel's" threat to reopen the impeachment scandal—avowing that the only reason he delayed doing so now was out of consideration for Hopkinson's growing family (1 April). Hopkinson did not reply, but even that could not spare him. Somebody signing himself "C. D." let fly a barrage of abusive epithets that must have reminded readers of the days when Hopkinson suffered the slings of Rivington's *Gazette* or Andrew Steuart's hackwriters the previous decade. "C. D." called "Franky's low pimping methods" natural in a homosexual deviate—"called sometimes *the mustard grinder, Franciani, Franky, the exquisite fiddler,* &c. &c. &c." Having flayed his morals, "C. D." turns to his tiny physical features—his "*frosty sheer-water face* might designate him a species of Ouran-Outang, or at least one of the large American monkies"—strip him of his outer garb and "'behold good people' the long *armed monkey* in his own dirty pelt" (3 April). Hopkinson could only sigh: "Scarcely a Day passes without my appearance in the Newspapers in every scandalous Garb that scribbling Vengeance can furnish."[1]

He immersed himself in designing and producing the "Grand Federal Procession" staged in Philadelphia on 4 July to celebrate both the ratification of the Constitution and the twelfth anniversary of the Declaration of Independence. This was a spectacular parade with marching units from all trades and professions, along with floats symbolic of their occupations and patriotism. The float representing "The Constitution" was a wagon 20 feet long, with wheels 8 feet high, decorated as an eagle and carrying all members of the state's supreme court except the die-hard anti-Federalist nabob, Justice George Bryan.

In token of Judge Bryan's absence perhaps, or out of sheer high spirits, Hopkinson wrote a satiric description of a "Grand Antifederal Procession" led by Bryan and featuring such stellar anti-Federalist

1. Hastings, p. 406.

performers as Eleazar Oswald and of course Benjamin Workman, who wore a dunce cap inscribed "Mens insana in Corpore sano" and delivered the post-parade oration, the same oration that had concluded the "New Roof."[2] As in earlier days, Hopkinson refrained from publishing this satire. Now, however, his reticence came less from fear of reprisal than from a realization that there was no longer a need for it.

With ratification of the Constitution in June, the anti-Federalists had tried to make one last stand, convening a conference at Harrisburg to muster support for another Constitutional Convention. There in September they succeeded only in passing resolutions calling for amendments. The preamble to these resolutions recognized "the federal constitution" as signaling "a new era in the American world." Though "Centinel" would continue his essays right down to the first national election day in November, his intent now was to sway voters to elect sufficient Congressional representatives to ensure a loyal opposition. By September, then, even the anti-Federalists accepted the fact that the United States had achieved the goal foretold fourteen years earlier in the *Pretty Story*. A prophet vindicated by time, Hopkinson once more donned the guise of the "Projector" to ruminate on a ready and easy way to preserve sanity in the sound body politic so arduously achieved.

## *Some Thoughts on the Diseases of the Mind; with a Scheme for purging the moral Faculties of the good People of Pennsylvania —quite new and very Philosophical.*

That there is an intimate connection between the soul and the body, and that the one is apt to be affected by the disorders and irregularities of the other, is a truth too manifest to be controverted. How this connection is formed, to what extent it exists, and what are the visible organs of the body, which compose the intermediate links of union with the invisible faculties of the mind, are problems which have been often in vain attempted. I neither pretend to have found out the secret, nor have I, at present, any plausible hypothesis to propose on this delicate subject.

This mutual influence, however, which plainly exists between

2. George Hastings, "Francis Hopkinson and the Anti-Federalists," *American Literature*, 1 (1929–30), 413–17.

spirit and matter in all animals, and more especially in man, hath produced many promising devices for remedying the disorders of the mind, which seem to be beyond our reach, by attacking the organs of the body, which are always within our power. A late ingenious author has gone great lengths in this hypothesis, in his dissertation on *the effects of physical causes on the moral faculty.*[3]

For my own part, I believe there is some truth in the doctrine, and that in particular cases, if applied with great judgment, a partial and temporary effect may be obtained. But if the seat of the disease should really be in the mind, it will be in vain to expect a *radical* cure by medical attacks on the body, which can do no more than, for the present, deprive the mind of the instruments by which she exhibits her distempered faculties.—For instance, suppose a person to be of an irascible captious disposition, and subject to violent and ungovernable gusts of passion. To reduce his body by phlebotomy, emetics, cathartics, a slender regimen, &c. would probably produce a dejection of spirits and apparent coolness of temper—but must this man be kept all his life time in a state of debility. For there is no doubt but as soon as health and vigour are allowed to return, the angry dispositions will return too, and perhaps with encreased inveteracy on account of the restriction. So also, if I should be infected with a troublesome itch for *scribbling*—which Heaven forbid!—and my friends, with a view to a cure, should deprive me of pen, ink and paper—for the present, to be sure, I could not scribble—but would the itch be removed? —Far from it—the scribbling matter being refused a discharge would accumulate and become more virulent—and as soon as the necessary instruments or organs of exhibition could be procured, I should scribble worse than ever.

This scheme of whipping the mind over the body's shoulders will not, I apprehend, answer any permanent purpose, and I know of no well authenticated cases to support the doctrine. Has government ever cured a propensity to theft by the administration

3. Benjamin Rush, *Enquiry into the Influence of Physical Causes upon the Moral Faculty* (1786).

of the whipping-post or wheel-barrow?[4] Amongst the innumerable experiments that have been made, I never heard of one successful instance.—No—It seems more natural, that mental remedies should be prescribed for mental disorders, and corporeal physic for bodily diseases. Let there be physicians and metaphysicians, as two distinct professions. I do not mean by *metaphysicians,* such as are now professors in universities and colleges, but *practising metaphysicians,* who shall study the disorders and irregularities of the human mind, and prescribe for their cure.

I have considered this matter very attentively, and am confident that many of the cares and evils of life might be removed or alleviated by a judicious metaphysical treatment. The first difficulty would be to gain the confidence of the patient in a new science; for this confidence would be as necessary to the metaphysical as it is to the physical cure of diseases; and even more so; for the imagination would have a great share in the business, and must indeed serve as apothecary to the metaphysician.—Wherein does the virtue of pills, potions and plaisters principally consist?—surely not so much in the ingredients of which they are composed, as in the implicit faith of those to whom they are administered. A proof of which is, that no sooner is the composition generally known, but it sinks into general contempt—no body will take a detected nostrum. If then this confidence, this implicit faith of the patient, is so useful in the operations of *material* medecine, much more should it be depended upon and cultivated in a *metaphysical* treatment.—Possessed of this, I could, with flattering hopes of success, attack the maladies of the mind, by the use of discreet and obviously rational means.

For instance—should I find my patient disposed to melancholy, and his mind clouded with imaginary doubts, difficulties and fears, by poring over polemic divinity—I would prescribe a round of amusements, much company, and frequent changes of companions; I would by every artifice provoke him to frequent laugh-

---

4. This had been the burden of another of Dr. Rush's pamphlets: *Enquiry into the Effects of Public Punishments* (1787).

ter, and plunge him deep into the vanities of this wicked world—but they should be vanities only; for I would on no account violate the bounds of strict morality.

To a patient of a contrary cast—vain, fickle, loquacious and full of levity, I would forbid the most innocent recreations—I would order him to take a chapter of the history of the martyrs every morning before breakfast—he should study algebra till dinner time—in the evening he should hear a long dull sermon, badly delivered, and should himself read one of our acts of Assembly before going to bed—and I would continue my Regimen and remedies, with a few judicious intermissions, until I saw an entire change of disposition take place, and a radical cure obtained.

But I am preparing a full account of the diseases of the mind, with the proper mode of treatment in each, illustrated by a variety of cases. This work hath cost me much study, and deep researches into human nature, and the subtile springs and movements of the moral faculty. Although my book is almost ready for publication, yet the evils of the present time call so loudly for redress, that I cannot delay giving an extract from my chapter on the *epidemic* diseases of the mind, in hopes it may be of immediate use.

"CACOETHES MALEDICTIONIS, or an insatiable rage for slander and abuse. This disease is peculiar to free governments. The proximate causes are envy, discontent, and an over-weening ambition; the diagnostic symptoms are an inveterate hatred of men of wealth or abilities, and particularly of those in public offices, and an unusual predominance of party spirit—and the crisis of the distemper is an acrimonious eruption, discharging a deal of prurient matter in private companies or in the public papers. The curative indication is manifest; for this, like many other mental diseases, is best managed by allowing a free emission to the peccant humours, and permitting the moral faculty to purge itself by natural discharges of the malevolent ichor."

This quotation suggests an observation or two which will lead directly to my present purpose.—It is recommended that the moral faculty should be suffered *to purge itself by natural dis-*

*charges*—Now there are but two possible ways by which the mind can discharge its contents in the *cacoethes maledictionis,* viz. by *actions* or *words*. The most natural and least dangerous vent is that of words; either by speaking, scolding, storming, swearing, writing or publishing; when these means are forbid or not conveniently obtained, the disease breaks into action, viz. beating, bruising, mawling, cuffing, kicking, and even murdering, killing, and so forth. And therefore a free scope should be given to *words,* as the most salutary and safe issue of the malignant matter.

The art of printing has been a great blessing to mankind, in as much as it affords a most convenient opportunity for the people to discharge their minds of indigested crudities, and rankling spleen. Before this invention, murders, assassinations, rebellions and revolutions were much more frequent than since. The poisoned cup and the bloody dagger are not known in countries where the press and the free use of it are allowed.—As this is a new and a very deep remark, I hope it will be attended to—I know that the less sanguinary character of modern ages has been attributed to the progress of civilization—but how has this civilization been advanced—certainly, by the vent which the press affords for the morbid minds of the people to get rid of their impurities, and the opportunity of keeping up a free circulation of ideas, so necessary to the mental health of man—As a proof, we see that in countries where free access to the press is not permitted, the *stilletto* is even at this day in use.

I now come to make the proposal which I had first in view when I sat down to write this paper, a proposal which I flatter myself will correct all the bad effects of party spirit or of personal animosity in this our city; and will sweeten and purify the political atmosphere of our commonwealth. The preface to this my project is I confess rather long; but it was necessary, to shew the metaphysical grounds upon which it is founded.

Let there be two public papers instituted—the one a weekly and the other a daily paper—let the printers be commissioned by government, and allowed competent salaries for their time and trouble. They should be *commissioned,* because all other printers should be prohibited from interfering in their department.—One of these papers may be entituled the ***** ****, and the other the **** ****. Let these offices be always open, as places where the good people of Pennsylvania may *ease* their minds without restraint, rebuke, or any hindrance whatever. And whereas some men are naturally bashful, and do not like to be seen in doing their occasions, there shall not only be fictitious signatures provided for their concealment, but the printer shall, for the purpose of decency, have a tin plate fixed in his window, fronting on a little alley, if his situation will permit, otherwise, on the street; in which tin plate there shall be a slit or opening, large enough to receive secretly any excrementitious matter—and it shall, for distinction's sake, be thus inscribed—"WHA WANTS ME?"—Lastly, the printers, their papers and their authors, should be *outlawed.* That is, they should be considered as beyond the reach of any censure or penalty of common or statute law, or restrictions by any ordinance, proclamation or regulation whatever.

By this institution all our other public papers would be kept free from impurities, and occupied, as they ought to be, with interesting or amusing articles of intelligence, grave or humorous essays, advertisements, &c. and all the filth of the city would be carried off by the commissioned papers. So that, after a little time, it would become as shocking to good manners for a man to vent his spleen in one of the public *news* papers, properly so called, as it would be to commit an indecent evacuation in a private parlour, or a public assembly. And thus, also, would the minds of the people be kept sweet and healthy; for we may refine as we will, but the mind certainly has her indecencies as well as the body, and when overloaded with indigested matter must have vent somewhere; for nature will be obeyed, and surely good policy requires that a suitable place should be provided for the purpose, rather than that the public sense should be offended by the evacuations of every distempered mind; which, though necessary, is neither decked with roses nor perfumed with amber.

Yet I would not exclude from the common papers of the city

attempts at wit or satire, or little effusions in verse in the poets corner. A sarcasm is nothing more than spitting—and so it is usual to say—"I have now spit my spite;"—a crude attempt at humour is parallel to blowing one's nose, for such humours are apt to collect in cold constitutions; and a young poetaster may be put into a considerable perspiration by the scorching flames of beauty—these may all happen in the best company without offence, provided they are conducted with decency; and they are certainly necessary to health.

I shall conclude with two instances in proof of my general system.

I knew a young man, about 32 years of age, of a slender habit of mind, who, from losses in trade and crosses in love, began to grow melancholy, retired and discontented. He came to me for advice. I asked him if he had ever tried to write verses. He answered, that he had upon two or three occasions, and found he could tack rhymes together pretty well, but had no thoughts of cultivating the talent. But I advised him by all means to do it. He followed my prescription, and for a year or two employed himself in writing Sonnets to Delia, Odes to Liberty, and Elegies on Squirrels, Birds and dead Lap-dogs—with a variety of other subjects, according to the course of the humours that infected his mind. He is now of a calm contemplative habit, but far from melancholy; on the contrary, he is delighted with his own performances, and enjoys the comfort of *self applause,* which, after all, is the most substantial comfort of life.

My second instance is that of a German doctor, who has had, or thinks he has had, a vision, in which the mysteries and œconomy of the spiritual world were manifested to him. He has told me the story of his vision, and a very long story it is—I heard it all with patient attention. Some time after, he wanted to tell me the same story over again, but I begged to be excused. Upon which he candidly assured me, that he found it absolutely necessary to relate the history of his vision at least once a week, otherwise he grew restless and uneasy in his mind.—He came indeed full up to my present system, and said, in *direct* terms, that it was *a necessary evacuation of his mind.*

The practice of the law affords, I confess, a convenient outlet for much mental virulence. Not only what are called *spite actions,* but many of those of a more sober aspect, are only extravasations of mental bile. But this process is too expensive and too tedious for general use. My proposal is I think much better in every respect. It is a scheme by which envy and revenge may be gratified without danger, and without cost; and abuse, slander and invective spend themselves, like rockets, in harmless explosions. For no man will ever think of giving credit to any thing contained in the ***** **** or the **** ****

PROJECTOR.

*Pennsylvania Gazette 17 September 1788.*